SINGAPORE AND UNICEF

Working for Children

World Scientific Series on Singapore's 50 Years of Nation-Building

---

The complete list of titles in the series can be found at
http://www.worldscientific.com/series/wss50ynb

World Scientific Series on
Singapore's 50 Years of Nation-Building

SINGAPORE AND UNICEF
Working for Children

Editors

Peggy Kek
Penny Whitworth

World Scientific

NEW JERSEY · LONDON · SINGAPORE · BEIJING · SHANGHAI · HONG KONG · TAIPEI · CHENNAI · TOKYO

Published by

World Scientific Publishing Co. Pte. Ltd.
5 Toh Tuck Link, Singapore 596224
USA office: 27 Warren Street, Suite 401-402, Hackensack, NJ 07601
UK office: 57 Shelton Street, Covent Garden, London WC2H 9HE

Library of Congress Cataloging-in-Publication Data
Singapore and UNICEF : working for children / edited by Peggy Kek, Penny Whitworth.
    pages cm. -- (World Scientific series on Singapore's 50 years of nation-building)
    ISBN 978-9814730808 (hardcover) -- ISBN 978-9814730815 (pbk.)
    1. UNICEF. 2. Child welfare--International cooperation. 3. Child welfare--Developing countries.
4. Humanitarian assistance, Singaporean. 5. Volunteer workers in child welfare--Singapore.
I. Kek, Peggy, editor. II. Whitworth, Penny, editor.
    HV703.U4766S56 2015
    362.7--dc23
                                            2015035150

British Library Cataloguing-in-Publication Data
A catalogue record for this book is available from the British Library.

Disclaimer
The contents of this book reflect the views of the contributors and do not necessarily reflect the views of the United Nations Children's Fund and any other organisation.

In-house Editor: Li Hongyan

Typeset by Stallion Press
Email: enquiries@stallionpress.com

Message

I congratulate Peggy Kek and Penny Whitworth for having edited an inspiring book on the UNICEF-Singapore story. It is a story that involves many characters performing different roles in various settings around the world over several decades.

The United Nations (UN) was founded 70 years ago. A year later, UNICEF was born. The original mandate was to help the children of Europe, a continent devastated by a ruinous war. The mandate was subsequently expanded to cover the entire world. The name was also changed to the UN Children's Fund but the acronym, UNICEF, was retained because of its brand equity.

Of the many institutions in the UN family, UNICEF is one of the best. Its focus on the well-being of children and their mothers is compelling. It is a lean organisation with highly motivated and committed staff and a global network of enthusiastic volunteers and partners.

Singapore was very poor at the end of World War II. The children suffered from malnutrition and many diseases. UNICEF was a life saver. It funded programmes to feed malnourished children with milk and cod liver oil and inoculate our children against five major diseases. UNICEF also played a seminal role in helping Singapore to develop its childcare and early education programmes.

Singapore's financial contributions to UNICEF have been modest. The people of Singapore, especially the students and young Singaporeans, have contributed more generously to UNICEF than the Government. Singapore does not have a National Committee for UNICEF. Instead, what we have is a small community of capable and committed Singaporeans, mostly women, who have worked for UNICEF. Individuals such as Ng Shui-Meng, Khoo Kim Choo, Cheng Wing-Sie and Peggy Kek deserve our respect and admiration. As they pursued and continue to pursue their meaningful careers across the globe, they help to reflect a light back on our Little Red Dot, showing the world how creative, honest, hardworking and professional Singaporeans can be.

Recently the INTERPOL was persuaded to establish a new campus in Singapore, focusing on cyber crime and cyber security, to take advantage of Singapore's knowledge and expertise, its strategic location and its multiculturalism.

UNICEF too has considered re-opening an office of some form here, but to-date, for various reasons the proposals have not become reality. I continue to hope that, when the time is ripe, UNICEF and Singapore will revisit the idea of setting up a presence in our country again.

Finally, I would like to commend this book to Singaporeans to read about how some of their own countrymen and UNICEF are helping to make the world a safer and better place for vulnerable children and mothers. I also recommend this book to those who are interested in the development and humanitarian aspects of the work of the UN.

Ambassador Tommy Koh
Singapore
1 October 2015

Tommy Koh is Ambassador-at-Large at the Ministry of Foreign Affairs. He has served as Singapore's Permanent Representative to the United Nations and chaired the UN Conference on Environment and Development (Earth Summit) in Rio de Janeiro in 1992.

Foreword

Since 1950, when UNICEF's then Executive Director Maurice Pate first met with the Commissioner-General of Singapore to discuss ways to promote the well-being and the rights of South-East Asian children, both UNICEF and Singapore have changed enormously.

Then, Singapore had not yet achieved independence, and UNICEF's support was needed to help overcome poverty and improve the health and well-being of Singaporean children. In the many years since, we have witnessed Singapore's independence and its emergence as a powerful and wealthy state. Today, Singapore has a great deal to offer its children, its neighbours and the world.

I am pleased to welcome you to *Singapore and UNICEF: Working for Children* — an account of the long road that UNICEF and Singapore have travelled together. The book offers many insights into children's issues in Singapore and other countries, mainly in the East Asia and Pacific region. The material its editors have gathered includes personal notes, official documents, press articles, interviews and oral anecdotes, along with images and memorabilia. The stories they illustrate are an excellent source of information about the many ways a strong partnership can be built for children.

We can learn a great deal that is both interesting and inspiring from this material. The interaction between Singapore and UNICEF has influenced the development of social welfare services for children in Singapore. Experiences such as those described in this book have also informed UNICEF's regional and global policies and programming strategies.

Much has been achieved for children in Singapore and around the world over the past 65 years although our task is far from over. The Convention on the

Rights of the Child — the most widely ratified human rights treaty in human history — establishes that every child, everywhere, must be protected, nurtured and respected. This is a global priority and a global responsibility. Singapore became a signatory to the Convention in 1995, and until every child can count on every right, UNICEF's work and Singapore's work will continue.

In September 2015, the United Nations General Assembly approved a new road map for action and cooperation to ensure the rights of every child and every person. The Sustainable Development Goals — the SDGs — are a promise by leaders to all people everywhere for shared prosperity, peace and partnership. Singapore can play an enormous role in the achievement of these goals, and UNICEF looks forward to working together with Singapore to that end.

This book casts light on the past with a view to the future. I hope it will inspire you to take action to make our world a safer and a better place for all children.

Finally, allow me to congratulate the Government and the people of Singapore on the occasion of your jubilee and to wish you good fortune as you continue to turn your dreams — and those of children everywhere — into reality.

Daniel Toole
UNICEF Regional Director
for East Asia and the Pacific
Bangkok, Thailand
6 October 2015

Contents

Preface

November 2014 marked 25 years since the adoption of the United Nations Convention on the Rights of the Child, the most widely ratified human rights treaty in history. In 2015 Singapore celebrates its Golden Jubilee, and in 2016 the United Nations Children's Fund (UNICEF) marks its 70th anniversary. The confluence of these milestones provided a happy occasion for the book.

From the Boy Scouts who sold UNICEF Christmas cards in the 1950s to the appointment of a Singaporean as Representative of a UNICEF country office in 2004, the people of Singapore have had a long and manifold engagement with UNICEF over the decades. The nature of the association evolved over time as Singapore's socio-economic circumstances changed. The multi-dimensional aspect of the relationship echoes UNICEF's connections with society in many countries elsewhere.

When we were working in the UNICEF Singapore office in the early 1990s, we were frequently invited to speak to different audiences about children in difficult circumstances and what was being done to help and protect them. We were asked about how ordinary people could contribute more to the work of UNICEF. We hope this book will help to provide some further answers and, perhaps, some inspiration.

The experiences of Singaporeans who live overseas and work in UNICEF field offices, helping to make a better world for vulnerable children, are little known by their compatriots at home. Their experiences typify those of many UNICEF staff working around the world, and deserve to be better known. Perhaps their stories will nudge other citizens of the Little Red Dot to consider a career with an international humanitarian and development agency.

This volume will appeal to anyone who is interested in development and the work of humanitarian organisations including students, professionals, specialists and the general public in Singapore and abroad.

We have spent deeply satisfying years working with UNICEF and with Singaporeans. We wanted to acknowledge this privilege and pay tribute to the organisation, our colleagues and the friends we made in the course of our work.

Peggy Kek
Penny Whitworth
15 September 2015

Acknowledgements

We would like to extend our profound gratitude to the following people for their considerable contributions in the research and writing of this book. We name below only some of the many individuals who actively participated in the compilation of this history. *Singapore and UNICEF: Working for Children* could not have been written without the co-operation and tireless work of staff and volunteers who have committed their energy to benefit children.

Special thanks to UNICEF Regional Director, Daniel Toole, and Ambassador-at-Large, Tommy Koh for their encouragement and contributions.

This is by no means a definitive account. Information has been sourced in archives from UNICEF Headquarters and publicly available online, Margaret Black's two historical accounts of UNICEF, the National Library Board's Digital Library, and various local Societies in Singapore.

Most importantly, a large part of the information presented here has come directly from those who were involved at the time. These personal accounts add substance and essence to the published facts and statistics. It is through these accounts that this becomes a memoir and a narrative. Some parts of the history are better remembered than others, other parts of the story have received less mention, if only because personal accounts were harder to come by. The chapters may not be the expressed opinions of UNICEF, nor may they represent unanimous consent on any particular event.

We are deeply grateful to all those who generously contributed their memories, analysis, photographs, time and editing skills. Their contributions were the high point in putting this project together. From their homes and offices around the world, retired and current UNICEF staff, consultants and volunteers have been willing to recall parts of a common history.

Our sincerest appreciation also goes to the following who helped us with information and photos: Margaret Theravakom of Singapore International Foundation; Cristene Chang, Lee Hock Moh, Quek Tse-Kwang, Yulian Ardhi, Lindy Poh of Silver Rue Art Consulting; Joy Loh of Eagle's Eye Art Gallery; Glendon Goh of Art Tree Gallery; staff of the UNICEF Regional Office for East Asia and the Pacific (EAPRO); Lisa Adelson-Bhalla, Dinia del Sol and Elizabeth Gladstone of UNICEF.

We want to thank Max Phua, Li Hongyan, Jimmy Low and Vanessa d/o Sundrasagar at World Scientific Publishing for their guidance throughout the process, and Leong Wen Shan, our indispensable copy editor.

Special mention must be made for the efforts and support of our family, friends and partners, and of Gillian Koh, whose belief in our book provided that all-important first nudge.

It has been a joyous endeavour.

Thank you all.

Introduction: Singapore and UNICEF Working for Children

Peggy Kek and Penny Whitworth

Finally, Mr President, though we are a small country not endowed with ample natural resources and though we cannot be counted among the highly advanced nations of the world, we are nevertheless a highly urbanised community that has acquired experience and knowledge which we are prepared to share with others in the regional cooperation schemes organised by the agencies of the UN. Undoubtedly these offers of assistance can be carried out only on a modest scale but if we obtain help from others, we must be ready to help others as much in return.

This is what the United Nations means to us and despite the cynics who focus attention on its many shortcomings, my country has faith in the future of the United Nations simply because without it there is no worthwhile future for humanity.

S. Rajaratnam
September 21, 1965[1]

With those words from the Foreign Minister, Singapore was admitted into the United Nations in 1965.

In the aftermath of World War II, in December 1946, UNICEF was established as the United Nations International Children's Emergency Fund to provide food, shelter and healthcare for the children of Europe and Asia. By 1950, the United Nations General Assembly had broadened the Fund's focus to "peace-time pro-gramming for children, particularly long-term programmes and services in

---

[1] From *50 Years of Singapore and the United Nations* by Tommy Koh and Li Lin Chang (2015, p. xix), "Excerpt from the statement delivered by S. Rajaratnam, then Foreign Minister of Singapore, to the UN General Assembly on 21 September 1965, on the occasion of Singapore's admission to the UN".

developing countries". The organisation was renamed the United Nations Children's Fund while its well-known acronym was retained.

UNICEF provided assistance to Singapore in its developing years, even before it gained independence, and also operated an office there for a substantial number of years after the assistance programmes had ended.

True to Mr Rajaratnam's words, UNICEF was one of the UN agencies to which Singapore would make both financial and in-kind contributions to help share its development experience with other countries.

How can aid agencies continue to engage beneficiary countries when the latter no longer need their help? How can and do countries that have benefited from aid give back? Beyond the official Basic Agreements of Cooperation signed between UN agencies and governments, what other connections do these agencies develop with the people of the country?

This book hopes to answer these questions through the lens of the relationship between UNICEF and Singapore. In different periods over the last 50 years, UNICEF has operated an office, in different forms, in Singapore. Over the years, several international officers of different nationalities have been based, for varying lengths of time, in the UNICEF office in Singapore. So while it is true that as we write this introduction today in 2015, there is no physical UNICEF presence in Singapore, there has always been a relationship over the last 50 years or so. It is a unique and multi-layered relationship that has emerged over the decades, as Singapore developed economically and UNICEF's programming and funding priorities evolved.

The chapter "A Brief History" provides an overview of the history of UNICEF's engagement with Singapore from the time it was still a territory under British rule to the confident republic it has grown into today.

The first section, **UNICEF in the Field: Singaporeans in Action**, features accounts of field experiences by Singaporean UNICEF staff and consultants spanning over three decades and several countries. They highlight innovative solutions that were used by UNICEF in nutrition, health, women's development and early childhood education to bring about improvement in the lives of children and young people in China, Laos, Nepal, Romania and Timor-Leste. They also explain some of the positions that UNICEF took on issues such as breastfeeding and HIV-AIDS.

The second section, **UNICEF Internationals in Action in Singapore**, pieces together the history of the period from the late 1980s through to the early 2000s when international staff from a range of nationalities were based in the UNICEF office in Singapore. Complementing the earlier accounts of field work by Singaporeans, these essays provide insights into other aspects of UNICEF that go into supporting the field work — namely, fundraising and the functions related to the much admired and studied UNICEF Greeting Card Operation. The writers describe how the UN agency made the most of Singapore's advantages and managed the limitations.

Throughout the world, wherever it operates, UNICEF has always been supported by the many willing hands of volunteers. Singapore was no different. From providing encouragement to breastfeeding mothers to showcasing UNICEF posters in a restaurant, from organising a charity film premiere to selling Christmas cards, the authors in the section **Volunteer Action in Singapore** vividly illustrate how they found creative ways, through their businesses and passions, to help and sustain the work of UNICEF in Singapore. How local artists also played their part is in the essay, "The Art of Giving". The essays situated in the 1990s when UNICEF local outreach was at its peak, paint a picture of the inspiring depth and breadth of the commitment and the talent to be found in the small city-state.

The book draws to a close with a few **Reflections** by former and current UNICEF staff on their careers with UNICEF and the changes they have seen in the organisation over the years.

Although this volume is not meant as an exhaustive record, we hope that researchers interested in the subject will find the data and accounts useful. The essays and interviews together will give a sense of the many connections that form the colourful tapestry of a rich and mutually benefitting relationship between Singapore and UNICEF, working for children around the world.

A Brief History of UNICEF in Singapore

Peggy Kek

During the final meeting of UNRRA (United Nations Relief and Rehabilitation Administration) held in Geneva in 1946, voices were raised about the fate of Europe's children. Ludwik Rajchman, the delegate from Poland, was particularly vocal, and the meeting accepted his proposal that UNRRA's residual resources be put to work for children through a United Nations International Children's Emergency Fund — an "ICEF". Rajchman is regarded, therefore, as the founder of UNICEF.

On 11 December 1946, the global community proclaims a new ethic of protection and care for children, establishing the United Nations International Children's Emergency Fund (UNICEF) to respond to the millions of displaced and refugee children deprived of shelter, fuel and food in the aftermath of World War II.

From *1946–2006: Sixty Years for Children*, p. 5

The historical accounts provide many insights into how UNICEF came into being, how its name was eventually changed and how the first Executive Director, Maurice Pate, had accepted the assignment only on condition that the organisation would be able to support children in all the countries, regardless if they had won or lost in the war.

Although UNICEF was initially established to feed the malnourished children of Europe, and was supposed to operate only till 1950, when UNICEF aid had reached most parts of Europe's war-devastated countries, the UN General Assembly recognised the need to reach out to other parts of the world where millions of children were suffering not just from the effects of war, but also the equally destructive consequences of poverty. In 1953, UNICEF was renamed the United Nations Children's Fund (but kept its acronym) and became a permanent fixture of the UN system.

1940s–1950s: Starting with Health and Nutrition

When UNICEF came into being in 1946, Singapore had just returned to British rule after a period of Japanese Occupation during WWII. In 1948, a decision had been taken to include the British-administered territories in Southeast Asia in UNICEF's programmes. In Maggie Black's very informative book, *UNICEF and the Nations*, she wrote about the first UNICEF mission to Asia.

> *In April 1948, in an attempt to try to establish a suitable policy for assisting in Asia, UNICEF invited two authoritative public health figures to undertake a survey of 13 Asian countries — Dr Thomas Parran, former Surgeon-General of the US Public Health Service, and Dr C. K. Lakshmanan, Director of the All-India Institute of Hygiene and Public Health in Calcutta. They travelled in British North Borneo, Burma, Ceylon, Hong Kong, India, Pakistan, Indo-China, Malaya, the Netherlands East Indies, the Philippines, Thailand and Singapore, meeting with senior health officials and trying to pinpoint child-health problems to which UNICEF's slender resources might be applied. In July they filed their report.*
>
> *Their first conclusion was that it would be impossible to attempt any large-scale feeding of hungry children.*
>
> From *UNICEF and the Nations* by Maggie Black, p. 71

Dr Parran and Dr Lakshmanan cited the large populations, shortage of "trained administrators" and "new and inexperienced governments" as some of the challenges in feeding the children. Taking note also of the high infant and child mortality rates, they decided to focus on child health. Assistance programmes for disease control were drawn up and they included supplying laboratory equipment, drugs, vaccines and training.

> *The high rate of infant death was striking in almost all the countries they visited. Only one country — Thailand — had a rate lower than 100 per thousand live births. Elsewhere, a rate of 200 was common, and in certain countries there were pockets where 300 was the norm.[1]*
>
> From *UNICEF and the Nations* by Maggie Black, p. 71

On April 11, 1950, UNICEF Executive Director Maurice Pate arrived in Singapore for a two-day visit for discussions, which would "include the planning of the future work of UNICEF in the British territories in South-East Asia."

Referring to his six-man mission, which included Director of UNICEF Operations in Asia, S.M. Keeny, and UNICEF Programme Coordinator Myron

---

[1] Singapore's rate was 75 in 1951 (when statistics became available).

Schmittlinger, Pate explained, "We are a mobile planning conference concerned with the work of UNICEF in Asian countries."

In June 1951, a BCG vaccination team arrived in Singapore:

> *The B.C.G. vaccination team under the auspices of the United Nations started their schedule in Singapore yesterday with T.B. tests for the pupils of the Convent of the Holy Infant Jesus.*
>
> *A public meeting will be held today at the British Council Hall to inaugurate the B.C.G. anti-tuberculosis campaign. Dr. Arne Buus-Hansen, Director of the joint B.C.G. team, will address the meeting and Dr. W.J. Vickers, Director of Medical Services will preside.*
>
> *The B.C.G. vaccination campaign is included in the United Nations International Children's Emergency Fund's allocation to Singapore of US$48,000. Other projects for Singapore children include the distribution of skimmed milk and the granting of fellowships to social and health workers.*
>
> From "B.C.G. team starts Singapore campaign",
> *The Straits Times,* June 4, 1951, p. 5

A month later, it was reported that 15,000 school children in Singapore had been inoculated against tuberculosis. And the team hoped,

> *... to start inoculating newborn babies at the Kandang Kerbau Maternity Hospital next month if the hospital can spare a doctor and nurses to learn the method, Dr Buus-Hansen said.*
>
> From "15,000 S'pore children get B.C.G.",
> *The Straits Times,* July 3, 1951, p. 4

By the end of their four-month stay in Singapore, the BCG team had tested 40,000 school-children, infants and newborn babies for tuberculosis and vaccinated half of them. The *Singapore Free Press* reported that these were carried out at KK Hospital and Infant Welfare Clinics in Singapore "where inoculations averaged 100 to 140 a day" and "at different rural areas where they averaged 61 children daily."

Dr. Buus-Hansen's team did not just carry out the vaccinations. They also trained a total of 12 doctors and 20 nurses to carry on the team's work. UNICEF's approach was to help strengthen local capacity and in addition to providing training within Singapore, it also awarded scholarships for overseas training. According to reports, UNICEF scholarships went to two nurses, Maude E. Pereira and Piong Eu Moi, to undergo training in the United Kingdom (UK). Another was given to Toh See King of the Social Welfare Department who also went to the UK to pursue a course on working with handicapped children. Each had the value of US$4,000 in 1951.

Milk, Milk, Milk

In 1953, UNICEF budgeted for Singapore to receive S$24,000 worth of milk and fish-liver capsules for undernourished mothers and children. Reports indicate that the milk programme was also an important component of UNICEF's aid to Singapore. The milk supplies were measured in pounds (lb.) and the amounts distributed carefully recorded.

In 1958, the Social Welfare Department said that UNICEF had distributed 39,285 lb. of milk in the April–June period and 37,745 lb. in the July–September quarter. The department estimated that 16,000 poor children had been brought into its feeding scheme with the help of UNICEF.

A December 1960 report showed that the "Social Welfare Department last month distributed 12,251 lb. of UNICEF milk to children's centres, crèches, hospitals and voluntary organisations." It was reported that "a total of 19,753 lb. of UNICEF milk" had been distributed in the last quarter of 1961.

These details were frequently reported in the media, so it is not surprising that many older Singaporeans today often associate UNICEF with the milk-feeding programme. An interesting account of the role of milk appears in a Singapore Children's Society book published in 2003.

> *To boost children's nutritional intake, they were encouraged to drink milk. Milk was not a typical component of the Asian diet but doctors and nutritionists at the time believed that it was the key to good health. The free milk programme had humble beginnings as a personal project by Dr J W Scharf, a government health officer, to introduce children in a rural school in 1936. Subsequently, from the end of the war up to the 1970s, the United Nations provided Singapore's needy and undernourished children with free milk, including skimmed milk and wheat soya blend. These supplies were distributed to the needy children through welfare institutions and schools.*
>
> From *Singapore Childhood: Our Stories Then and Now*
> by Jamie Koh and the Singapore Children's Society, p. 162

The Straits Times reported that between 1948 and 1958, UNICEF had spent nearly S$250,000 to help needy children in Singapore. The *New Nation* reported that UNICEF had "approved US$204,700 (S$ 491,280) in aid for Singapore from 1950 to 1972."

1960s–1970s: Assistance for Lasting Capacity Development

The statistics (available from 1951) showed that infant mortality rates had dropped steadily from 75.2 per 1,000 resident live births in 1951 to 26.3 per 1,000 resident live births in 1965. Maternal mortality rates also improved from 164 per 100,000 live and still births in 1951 to 39 per 100,000 live and still births in 1965.

Nineteen years after its creation, in 1965, UNICEF was awarded the Nobel Peace Prize for "fulfilling the condition of Nobel's will, the promotion of brotherhood among nations" and emerging on the world stage as "a peace-factor of great importance." In the same year, Singapore became a sovereign nation. UNICEF continued to support the city-state after independence.

In 1967, UNICEF donated S$40,000 to support Singapore's health education programme. In a *Straits Times* report, the Ministry of Health explained that UNICEF's donation was an additional source of help for the programme, which had received assistance from the World Health Organization (WHO) and had been in operation for many years:

> *UNICEF's assistance includes a fithopress, photographic projection, display and reproduction equipment and a public address van.... The Health Education Unit is an example of co-operation between the Government and the two international agencies. The planning and day-to-day work is being done by the government officers while WHO provides the technical advice and UNICEF the essential equipment.*
>
> From "UNICEF to donate $40,000 for health work",
> *The Straits Times*, 1967, July 16, p. 4

The *New Nation* reported that UNICEF had provided Singapore with aid of US$60,000 from 1973 to 1976. UNICEF assistance to the young country in the latter years took the form of supporting the training of social welfare personnel and research and project evaluation personnel. Thung Syn Neo, a pioneer in Singapore's social work profession, recalled that the Training and Research Section at the then Social Welfare Department had been set up with funding from UNICEF.[2]

In 1977, UNICEF provided funding support for the set-up of the People's Association-UNICEF Family Service Centre (FSC) in MacPherson constituency, located in the central part of Singapore. The project, launched in a small government-subsidised flat to bring its services "into the heart of the community", was

---

[2] Thung was inducted in the Singapore Women's Hall of Fame in 2014 for her contributions to social work. Details of her career can be found at http://www.swhf.sg/the-inductees/13-community-social-work/132-thung-syn-neo.

a pilot to "test methods and approaches and developmental welfare services with the participation of the local community and social services organisations."

Social welfare services that UNICEF assists include parent education with special attention to women and girls, neighbourhood and community centre programmes, day-care services, youth agencies, and women's clubs.

From *UNICEF Annual Report* 1977, p. 21

Thung recalls the process of chairing the planning committee and leading the team to develop the centre as a "highlight of her career". In a 1980 newspaper report of Parliament Debate Highlights, then Social Affairs Minister Dr Ahmad Mattar was quoted as saying that the children in MacPherson constituency had become "less inclined towards vandalism and fights" and that "[they were] more interested in their studies and show more respect towards family members." Today, there are more than 40 Family Service Centres in Singapore.

A *New Nation* journalist, Singaporean Edgar Koh (who would later go on to work for UNICEF in New York), writing from a special UNICEF meeting in Manila in May 1977, reported that Singapore, being "comparatively better off economically" was receiving UNICEF assistance that had "not strictly followed traditional lines, but… taken a pragmatic course." He went on to explain that UNICEF's strategy for Singapore was "to make preventive and developmental work the keynote of services as against the more traditional, remedial and residual aspects of social welfare" and that the approaches taken by the then Social Affairs Ministry in Singapore had been "partly inspired by UNICEF." Referring to a UNICEF report presented at the meeting, Koh wrote:

Reviewing past contributions, the report says UNICEF's assistance to health services, particularly the school health care, has played an important role in helping to maintain Singapore's "remarkable health record". Since 1971, the agency has assisted in problems of nutrition, particularly among pre-school children; screening of primary and secondary school entrants and leavers; dental care through 60 school dental clinics to 160,000 primary school children; a sight and sound centre set up in 1973 which discovered that 25% of students have defective eyesight; and the Health Ministry's Child Guidance Unit which provides treatment and psychiatric services for about 110,000 emotionally disturbed children.

From "UNICEF's task in Singapore",
New Nation, May 19, 1977, p. 9

Records seem to indicate that Singapore last received substantive financial assistance from UNICEF around 1977. Singapore continued to make inroads in the health and well-being of children. By 2000, the infant mortality rate had fallen to

2.5 deaths per 1,000 resident live deaths, that is, less than a tenth of what it was in 1965, while maternal mortality had dropped to less than half: 17 deaths per 1,000 resident live and still births. See Annex 1 for more details.

1970s–1980s: Progress and the Lighter Side

On October 28, 1971, American comedian and UNICEF Goodwill Ambassador Danny Kaye arrived in Singapore to make a film of school health services in South-East Asia. He visited Delta Circus Primary School where he joined the pupils in a teeth-brushing line, and entertained the pupils while they waited to undergo their health and dental check-ups. As UNICEF's original Ambassador, he was the first celebrity in history to advocate for a global cause. He travelled widely on behalf of UNICEF from 1954 until his death in 1987.

In 1974, Singapore issued a set of new stamps to mark Children's Day on October 1. The four stamps were the first in Singapore to feature drawings by children. The 10-cent and 35-cent stamps featured drawings by Angeline Ang and Si-Hoo Yeen Joong, respectively, both of Marymount Kindergarten. The five-cent and 50-cent stamps featured drawings by Chia Keng San of Khee Fatt Kindergarten and Raymond Teo of St Andrew's Kindergarten.[3]

In 1981, UNICEF featured the painting of a Singaporean artist, as part of the UNICEF/United Nations First Day Covers commemorating the UN Flag stamp series. This came about because of the friendship between James P. Grant, who was UNICEF Executive Director from January 1980 to 1995, and Tommy Koh who was then Singapore's Permanent Representative to the United Nations, New York. In an email to this book's editors, dated July 4, 2015, Koh explained:

> I was a good friend of the Executive Director of UNICEF. With his help I was able to introduce some of our best artists, such as Cheong Soo Pieng, Chen Wen Hsi, Tay Bak Koi and Tay Chee Toh to UNICEF. When they were looking for a painting from Singapore depicting the mother and child theme, I managed to get Soo Pieng to agree to allow UNICEF to use the image of this painting for the first day cover. I personally brought back many issues of the first day cover for Mr Cheong. He was very happy.

That First Day Cover featuring Cheong Soo Pieng's *Mother and Daughter* would pave the way for the works of other Singaporean artists to be discovered by UNICEF and featured on the greeting cards.[4]

---

[3] The stamps are featured in the photo section of this book.

[4] For details on Singapore artists and UNICEF greeting cards, see the chapter "The Art of Giving" in this volume.

UNICEF greeting cards were a constant throughout the history of UNICEF-Singapore relations. In the late 1950s and early 1960s, Singapore Boy Scouts and the Jaycees (the Junior Chamber of Commerce) sold UNICEF Christmas cards to help raise funds for UNICEF projects. Year after year they would try to break the previous record of money raised. In 1960, the cards were sold at S$3 for a box of 10 cards. According to *The Singapore Free Press*, Anthony Hee Koon Lim was then chairman of the Jaycees' UNICEF Cards Committee and made this plea:

> *Your contribution towards the purchase of one box of cards will go a long way in provid-ing 300 children with a glass of milk each. Five boxes will help to vaccinate 300 children against tuberculosis.*

From "Mercy Cards",
The Singapore Free Press, August 16, 1960, p. 4

The following year, the new Chairman of the Jaycees' UNICEF Cards Committee, Thio Tiong Wah, urged with a similar message: "If everyone in Singapore were to buy and send the cards during the holiday season, tens of thousands of these children would enjoy the benefits". That year, the cards carried designs by artists such as Pablo Picasso, Bedri Rahmi Eyuboghn, Ikhaluk, Mungituk and Andre François.

In the latter 1960s, the Singapore Council for Social Service took on the role of the promotion and sale of UNICEF cards. This was a role they played actively until the 1980s, when UNICEF opened its own office in Singapore.

Mid-1970s and 1985–2000: Singapore as a UNICEF Hub

In the 1970s the Indochina conflict caused great hardship to children as a result of damage to their schools and homes, separation from their families and physical harm from anti-personnel landmines. This created "the need for a large international effort to assist in rehabilitation and reconciliation," as pronounced by the 1973 annual report of UNICEF. The organisation used Singapore as a supply hub to facilitate quicker responses to neighbouring countries in need:

> *In order to be in a position to deliver assistance more rapidly once the government authorities have agreed on the projects to be assisted, UNICEF moved some stocks from the Copenhagen assembly and packing centres to Singapore. They include drug kits, midwives kits, light motor vehicles, bicycles, sewing machines, and some equipment for health centres and paediatric wards, to the value of US$ 1 million.*

From *UNICEF Annual Report 1973*, p. 23

In 1985, Guenter Duethorn, then chief of UNICEF's Greeting Card Operation (GCO) visited Singapore on a feasibility study, with colleague Kurt Rothlisberger, production and quality control officer. Duethorn was reported by *The Straits Times* as saying, "Singapore is the best location for our Asian base because of its central location, facilities and printing quality, among other things. Only the detailed cost estimates need to be assessed now." Kunio Waki, then Deputy Regional Director at the UNICEF East Asia and Pacific regional office in Bangkok, added: "Singapore is also favoured as the location because UNICEF wants to strengthen relations with the government of Singapore. The operations will also extend the outlook of people in Singapore to the needs of the children in Third World countries."

A year later, UNICEF set up a Greeting Card Operation (GCO) office in Singapore. The goal was to de-centralise the production and distribution of the greeting cards and other products to gain time and save costs. The essays in section 2 of this book, "UNICEF Internationals in Action: UNICEF in Singapore", written by UNICEF international staff who had been based in the Singapore office, provide detailed accounts of its operations. The move was also described in UNICEF's annual reports:

> *GCO, like any commercial enterprise, is affected by changing market conditions and requires operational autonomy to respond promptly to these changes.... GCO-managed offices have been established in Brazil, Colombia, India, Japan, Mexico and Singapore, which serve as sales and distribution centres for important markets that do not yet have strong voluntary support networks.*
>
> From *UNICEF Annual Report 1986*, p. 44

> *In order to provide the best products at the lowest price, GCO continued to expand local production activities in Brazil (for South and Central American countries) and in Singapore (for all countries in Asia and Pacific).*
>
> From *UNICEF Annual Report 1987*, p. 44

The office also took over the responsibility for card sales for the Singapore market and its opening ushered in a period of very special relations between UNICEF and the people of Singapore. Indeed as the office became more settled after a few years, volunteer participation, card sales revenues and donations peaked in the early to mid-1990s. Several essays in section 3 of this volume, "Volunteer Action in Singapore", describe many of the events, encounters and experiences associated with this time.

In addition to fundraising, there were educational and advocacy activities during this period. One instance was the seminar on the "Rights of a Child in the Next Decade" co-organised by the United Nations Association of Singapore and

UNICEF in 1988. It was held on 20 December to coincide with the launch of UNICEF flagship report, the *State of the World's Children Report* for 1989, open to "diplomats, teachers, students and representatives of several social and service organisations". Parliamentary Secretary (Foreign Affairs), Yatiman Yusof, was invited to grace the seminar.

Another close advocacy partner in the 1990s was the local Breastfeeding Mothers' Support Group (BMSG). Together UNICEF and BMSG collaborated to promote the Baby Friendly Hospital Initiative in Singapore. Lynette Thomas' essay in Section 3 of this book gives more details.

With changing technology, shifts in the global economy and a consolidation of the UNICEF product selection, the regional production centre in Singapore was phased out in 1994. In its place, a regional support centre was formed for the development and strengthening of fundraising and sales. A few years later, this function was consolidated in the regional offices of UNICEF in Bangkok and the office in Singapore was closed in early 2001.

Singaporeans give Back

It was also in the 1980s that Singaporean professionals joined the ranks of UNICEF's international staff. Among these were Edgar Koh, Cheng Wing-Sie and Ng Shui-Meng who served in postings from Nepal to New York. Wing-Sie and Shui-Meng write about their experiences in section 1 of this book, "Singaporeans in Action: UNICEF in the Field".

One of the striking things that emerged in our research was that Singaporeans did not wait till they had reached a certain level of economic status before giving back. Even while Singapore was receiving assistance in the 1950s, Singaporean Boy Scouts were selling UNICEF cards to help raise funds.

There were also contributions from the government of Singapore to UNICEF. The earliest record of these contributions was in 1971, when Singapore donated US$8,400. That year, Singapore was still receiving assistance from UNICEF. The government contributions stayed in the range of US$8,000 to US$13,000 until 1978. Then they dropped to US$1,400 in 1982, and stopped completely from 1983 until 1990.

From 1991 to 1995, the government of Singapore started making annual contributions again of US$10,000 from 1991 to 1995, doubling that to US$20,000 from 1996, and US$40,000 in 1997. From 1999, records showed that contributions were increased to US$50,000. Over the last 10 years, Singapore has consistently donated US$50,000 annually to the general budget of UNICEF. In the 2000s, the government also made additional donations of between US$10,000 to US$50,000 to the supplementary budget for special purposes such as for a water and sanitation programme in Gaza. In 2014, Singapore made an additional US$100,000 donation to the supplementary budget. (See Annex 2 for more details.)

Records of total contributions from non-government sources to UNICEF (including revenue from the sale of UNICEF greeting cards) exceeding US$10,000 are available from 1971. However there are no records of non-government contributions (NGC) from Singapore between 1971 and 1980. Since there were revenues from the UNICEF sales, the likely explanation for the lack of data is that the total contributions from donations and revenues did not exceed US$10,000. From 1981 modest contributions started at US$17,100 and rose to US$32,700 in 1987, a year after UNICEF opened an office in Singapore. Following that, the contributions gained momentum quickly and for the first time exceeded US$100,000 in 1991, when NGC totalled US$126,300. In 1992, the sale of cards and private donations had reached a peak of US$374,400 partly because of emergency appeals for Somalia. After the Singapore office closed in 2000, the NGC levels became somewhat erratic until 2006, followed by a period from 2007 to 2013, when there is no data available in the UNICEF annual reports. In 2014, there was a big jump of over US$240,000 of which US$100,000 was a contribution from the International Zinc Association and the rest derived from a cause-related marketing programme with the company Mont Blanc, known for its pens and leather accessories. (See Annex 2 for more details.)

The higher numbers reached in the 1990s may be accounted for by increased outreach from the UNICEF office and the high levels of involvement by volunteers.[5]

Ratifying the CRC and Post 2000

In November 1989, the United Nations General Assembly, taking into consideration that "the child, by reason of his physical and mental immaturity, needs special safeguards and care, including appropriate legal protection, before as well as after birth", adopted and opened for signature the Convention on the Rights of the Child (CRC). In 1995, the East Asia and the Pacific region achieved universal ratification of the CRC with the addition of Brunei, Kiribati, Malaysia, Palau, Solomon Islands, Tonga, Tuvalu and Singapore.

---

[5] For more on the involvement of volunteers, see essays in section 3 of this volume.

In its May 2011 report, the Committee on the CRC welcomed the measures that Singapore government had implemented to fulfil its obligations under the Convention.[6] Among others, these included the:

— amendment of article 122 of the Constitution in April 2004, allowing children to acquire citizenship through their Singaporean mothers
— ratification of the ILO Convention (No. 138) concerning Minimum Age for Admission to Employment in 2005
— amendment of the Penal Code in October 2007, which criminalises child sexual exploitation in Singapore and other countries

The Committee also expressed concerns in the areas where there were still deficiencies. These included the lack of a comprehensive national plan of action for the implementation of the convention, the inadequacy of data on violence against children, and the lack of clarity regarding cooperation with civil society at the policy-making level.

In 1999, UNICEF began collaborating with the Singapore Cooperation Programme (SCP) in training programmes on Early Children Development. As a small country whose key resource is its people, the Singapore government believes very much in human resource development and, in turn, prides itself in such transfers when contributing to the development agenda.[7] This is consistent with the approach taken by UNICEF — sharing best practices, experience and expertise, and training — where such capacity-building support is recognised as highly effective in putting countries on the road to self-sufficiency.

Between 1999 and 2005, the UNICEF-SCP partnership resulted in 10 courses and workshops for 211 government officials from 19 countries.[8]

Since UNICEF closed its office in Singapore in 2001, there have been some attempts to bring a UNICEF presence back. Overtures were made by both UNICEF and the Singapore government but differences in views over the man-

---

[6] Available in the Concluding Observations made by the Committee on the Rights of the Child at its Fifty-Sixth Session (17 January–4 February 2011).
[7] According to the Ministry of Foreign Affairs, Singapore, "One factor which helped Singapore's development is the valuable external help it received from other countries and international agencies in the early years of its development. It benefited from the training provided by them, and avoided their mistakes. In turn, Singapore shares its development experience with other nations…through the Singapore Cooperation Programme (SCP)."
[8] Dr Khoo Kim Choo writes more about this partnership in her essay in this volume.

date, structure and operations of the entity have still to be resolved. In the meantime though, collaboration continues between UNICEF and a range of organisations in Singapore.

In 2005, the Singapore International Foundation (SIF), which runs the Singapore International Volunteers programme (then known as Singapore Volunteers Overseas) placed a former Singapore journalist to help the UNICEF office in Timor-Leste with outreach. As a Communications consultant, Bridgette See wrote many stories about the children of Timor-Leste and UNICEF's efforts to improve their well-being. Many were published online by UNICEF.

In 2009, the UNICEF Regional Office for East Asia and the Pacific (EAPRO) convened a highly successful conference on the "Impact of the Economic Crisis on Children" with the Lee Kuan Yew School of Public Policy of the National University of Singapore, again with the support of the Singapore Ministry of Foreign Affairs. The Conference, assembled at a time when countries in the region were facing rising fuel and food prices, examined the crisis, its impacts on child health, education and family livelihoods, and explored possible responses. It was attended by some 150 participants from the region, from government, academia and civil society, including the Indonesian Finance Minister, the Singapore Minister for Community Development, Youth and Sports and then-UNICEF Regional Director Anupama Rao Singh.

Conclusion

Though not exhaustive, this brief history is a testament to the broad range of connections between Singapore and UNICEF that began in the late 1940s, continued, evolved and came full circle in the 1990s and 2000s when Singapore began supporting other countries in the region in a substantial and more formal way through the joint workshops in Early Childhood Development (ECD) and so on. The physical presence of an office and full-time staff did provide a huge impetus for collaboration, although the absence of a physical presence did not deter cooperation at the beginning nor cease after the office closed in 2000. Expertise exchange and project funding in relevant fields were initiated before and continued after the presence of an office. In the absence of an office, what does fall off though are opportunities for private citizens to have an active involvement in the international efforts to make the world a safer place for children to go to school and grow up to be healthy members of their communities.

Even as this book goes to print, the government of Singapore has pledged its commitment and support to the United Nations' 2030 Agenda for Sustainable Development which includes a set of Sustainable Development Goals. UNICEF and Singapore are also in talks to bring UNICEF back to the city-state in a more substantial way. Perhaps in the future, another chapter may be added to this history.

References

Koh, J. (2003). *Singapore Childhood: Our Stories Then and Now*. Singapore: World Scientific Publishing for the Singapore Children's Society.

New Nation. (1971, October 28). Danny gets a big welcome, p. 1.

New Nation. (1974, September 7). Work of kids for this special issue, p. 8.

New Nation. (1977, May 19). UNICEF's task in Singapore, p. 9.

The Singapore Free Press. (1951, September 27). B.C.G. Team's missions accomplished, p. 5.

The Singapore Free Press. (1958, October 31). 16,000 now get milk, too, p. 5.

The Singapore Free Press. (1959, August 10). Jaycees help UNICEF, p. 5.

The Singapore Free Press. (1960, August 16). Mercy Cards, p. 4.

The Singapore Free Press. (1960, September 19). Scouts will go all out to sell 20,000 UNICEF cards, p. 7.

The Singapore Free Press. (1960, December 14). Milk to Children, p. 13.

The Singapore Free Press. (1961, September 1). Jaycees get 100,000 UNICEF cards to aid the needy, p. 7.

The Singapore Free Press. (1962, February 24). 175,417 snacks supplied to children, p. 7.

The Straits Times. (1950, April 12). U.N. Mission in S'pore for talks with C.G., p. 8.

The Straits Times. (1951, June 4). B.C.G. team starts Singapore campaign", p. 5.

The Straits Times. (1951, June 5). S'pore Ahead of UK in BCG Campaign, p. 8.

The Straits Times. (1951, July 3). 15,000 S'pore children get B.C.G., p. 4.

The Straits Times. (1951, November 14). S'pore wants Unicef aid, p. 7.

The Straits Times. (1953, September 29). $165,000 to aid child welfare schemes, p. 7.

The Straits Times. (1958, November 17). A plea on behalf of children, p. 4.

The Straits Times. (1960, September 19). Sale of cards for Unicef, p. 4.

The Straits Times. (1967, July 16). UNICEF to donate $40,000 for health work, p. 4.

The Straits Times. (1967, September 23). UNICEF cards, p. 24.

The Straits Times. (1971, October 29). Danny gives the kids a big laugh, p. 20.

The Straits Times. (1980, March 26). Debate highlights, p. 10.

The Straits Times. (1985, August 7). Unicef to make festive cards in Singapore, p. 31.

The Straits Times. (1988, December 17). Unicef seminar to discuss the rights of children, p. 18.

Tower, S. A. (1981, September 13). Stamps: U.N. flag series continues. http://www.nytimes.com/1981/09/13/arts/stamps-un-flag-series-continues.html (retrieved on 2015, August 25).

UNICEF. (2009). Factsheet on Singapore-UNICEF Collaboration Under the Singapore Cooperation Programme (SCP). http://www.unicef.org/eapro/fact_sheet(final).pdf

UNICEF Annual Reports 1972–1999. http://www.unicef.org/about/history/index_annualreports.html

UNICEF Annual Reports 2000–2014. Available at www.unicef.org

Annex 1

Table on Infant and maternal mortality.

Year	Infant mortality rate (per 1,000 resident live births)	Maternal mortality rate (per 100,000 live and still births)
1951	75.2	164
1955	49.5	89
1960	34.9	45
1965	26.3	39
1970	20.5	32
1975	13.9	30
1980	8.0	5
1985	7.6	5
1990	6.6	2
1995	3.8	4
2000	2.5	17
2005	2.1	13
2010	2.0	3
2014	1.8	2

Source: Population and Vital Statistics, Ministry of Health, Singapore

Annex 2

Contributions from Singapore in US dollars

Year	Non-Governmental sources	Government
1971	NA	8,400
1972	NA	11,300
1973	NA	13,900
1974	NA	13,000
1975	NA	13,800
1976	NA	13,200
1977	NA	10,200
1978	NA	8,200
1979	NA	6,600
1980	NA	2,800
1981	17,100	1,100*
1982	20,763	1,400
1983	14,073	NA
1984	11,700	NA
1985	NA	NA
1986	NA	NA
1987	32,700	NA
1988	56,300	NA
1989	48,900	NA
1990	77,900	NA
1991	126,300	10,000
1992	374,400	10,000
1993	166,300	10,000
1994	277,981	10,000
1995	298,412	10,000
1996	220,118	20,000
1997	261,055	40,000
1998	NA	NA
1999	338,004	50,000
2000	69,151	50,000
2001	308,073	50,000

* This is an approximate number as the figure is partially obscured in the scanned annual report online.

(*Continued*)

(Continued)

Year	Non-Governmental sources	Government
2002	118,270	50,000
2003	46,500	50,000
2004	53,956	50,000
2005	47,687	60,000
2006	1,690	100,000
2007	NA	50,000
2008	NA	50,000
2009	NA	80,000
2010	NA	80,000
2011	NA	50,000
2012	NA	50,000
2013	NA	50,000
2014	243,564	150,000

Note: NA = Not Available.

Sources: UNICEF Annual Reports (1972–2014).

Section 1

Singaporeans in Action: UNICEF in the Field

Improving Children's Lives in Laos

Ng Shui-Meng with Peggy Kek[1]

Dr Ng Shui-Meng was the Education Officer in UNICEF Laos from 1989 to 1996, at a time when there was a dire lack of schools and trained teachers in the country, as well as a high incidence of malnutrition among children. She also worked on the Women's Development programme as the development of women was and continues to be closely tied to the welfare of children. During her tenure at UNICEF Laos, she and her team formulated a number of pragmatic solutions to meet urgent needs at the time, specifically in education and community development.

Making a Direct Impact with Untrained Teachers

When I first joined UNICEF Laos in 1989, both the Education and the Women's Development programmes were almost entirely dedicated to the capital, Vientiane, where our main partners — the government, the Ministry of Education and the Lao Women's Union — were based. The Ministry was mainly interested to get UNICEF to support its Teachers Training Colleges because they needed teachers. They also wanted UNICEF to support its toy factory because of UNICEF's interest and expertise in Early Childhood Development.

At the time, UNESCO[2] was operating out of Bangkok and working out a joint programme with UNICEF Laos. UNESCO was to provide the technical support and the pedagogical support. The programme involved printing books, distributing furniture for schools, and helping to put water and sanitation facilities in the Teachers Training Colleges.

---

[1] This account is based on an interview by Peggy Kek on 6 June 2015.
[2] United Nations Educational, Scientific and Cultural Organization.

This was all fine. But I felt we could do more to reach out more directly to the children out in the provinces. When I became the Education Officer, there was an opportunity for UNICEF to re-design its programme based on the findings of the situation analysis that I had done. In terms of education, the findings showed there was a dire lack of schools and trained teachers in Laos.

So we decided to reshape the programme. We moved away from providing hardware and supporting the work of other people, and started to chart new directions. I spent the first couple of years trying to understand how we could be more strategic.

One of the ways we did this was by going beyond teacher training into curriculum. Not having the technical capacity and having only limited resources, we worked closely with Save the Children UK and pooled our resources with them. Save the Children UK focused more on secondary level education, while we looked into the primary level.

There were so many untrained teachers. In the rural schools, they had only one or two trained teachers. Most of them had hardly finished high school, but were already assigned to teach.

As there were already other agencies providing training courses for teacher trainees, we decided to turn our attention on the untrained teachers who were already in the community. There was a real need to focus on them because they were already in the community and they were committed. Our programme was designed to fill an unmet need, a niche.

We worked with the Ministry to develop very pragmatic teacher training programmes for the untrained teachers: how to make training materials, how to teach in a classroom, and so on. They would come to receive training during the school holidays, and the training was very intensive. During regular school term, we worked with the Ministry and the provincial education leaders to train what we called the "teacher-educators", who followed the teachers and provided them with effective support.

This turned out to be very practical — putting UNICEF's resources where they were most needed and where there could be the quickest impact. When this teacher-upgrading programme was assessed by a team of independent education specialists contracted by the UNICEF Regional Office and evaluated, it was considered one of the most successful programmes in Laos.

Supporting Women Farmers to Benefit Early Childhood Development

For UNICEF Laos' Women's Development programme, again we focused on very practical things. The Lao Women's Union wanted us to build crèches and kindergartens and to help them in building up their systems, to support them in Vientiane. But we also wanted to see where the needs of the women with young children were outside of the capital. So we conducted village consultations. We then negotiated with the Union, so that while we would continue to provide some support to them in Vientiane, the bulk of our support would be in the provinces and districts.

We were able to move the emphasis of our work out from the capital to five provinces; two in the north, one in the centre and two in the south. We began working closely with the people at the provincial and district levels, trying to understand what the needs were at the local level.

What I found out very quickly was this: If you wanted to find out what the issues were, you could gather both the men and the women together to tell you. But the men faced slightly different issues from the women, so we also had gender-specific consultations.

With limited resources, we decided to focus on what the women themselves identified as key needs because they were the ones who ran the households, they were the ones responsible for feeding the children and so on. The women identified very practical needs, and we concluded that the women needed to be supported on two or three very basic things.

First, a lot of time was spent on pounding rice. It's very labour-intensive and physically arduous. The other thing was fetching water and firewood. So everywhere you went, you would hear women say, "I don't have time. It's not because I don't want to take better care of my children, I just don't have time." All that pounding was draining their energy. While they were mothers, they were also farmers.

So we concentrated on working at the community level, while still working very closely with the Women's Union. We put in very simple rice mills — rice husking machines that the village Women's Union committee could organise and run. They collected a small fee and freed the women from the labour of pounding rice.

Then we put in simple water and sanitation (WatSan) systems. Simple things like tube wells, hand-dug wells and pumps — again, to free the women, especially girls, from fetching water. UNICEF Lao's Women's Development programme worked very closely with our WatSan programme, putting our resources in the same places, geographically.

Second, we identified one of the biggest problems was food shortage during certain times of the year. Typically, the villagers suffered a lack of rice at the end of the rice production schedule — when they had eaten last year's harvest, their rice stock was depleted, but their new rice had not yet been harvested. So there was a period of about one to two months when they would run very low in rice. That's the time they would go and borrow rice from the rice merchants, who charged them very high interest. They would borrow one bag, or 50 kilogrammes of rice, and when their new rice was harvested, they would pay back two bags, or double what they borrowed.

After discussing with the women, we decided to set up rice banks, run by the Women's Union groups themselves, who then loaned the rice to the village women. They still had to pay interest, but the interest was 20 or 30%, which was much less than the 100% charged by the merchants. And because the local community ran the rice banks, they could give special dispensation to the very, very poor — those who could not afford to pay the rice loan.

In the meantime, we also worked with the women to help identify other production needs. Some women said they needed to grow more vegetables. So we provided practical support like vegetable seeds.

Whatever we did, we directed our efforts on the community, who ran the programmes themselves, and we always did so with an eye on building capacity.

We brought those things like water and sanitation close to them, so that they could save time. Otherwise, for instance, the women would not have time to take the children for immunisation. They often left the children alone at home while they were out busy doing what they were busy with. Young girls were also collecting water; once we freed up their time, they could also go to school.

By giving women more time to focus on their children, we were then able to address early childhood development. We focused on early childhood care, on breastfeeding, how to deal with children suffering from diarrhoea, and encouraging women to bring their children for immunisation and for play.

At any one time, there would be a few families in the community who would have a newborn, or a very young baby under the age of two. There were no kindergartens at the time, but we were able to train a few women cadres to work with the mothers to help them with their childcare. Having a home — not quite a childcare centre — where the mothers could gather and get some very basic information about childcare, e.g., sanitation, cleaning, feeding practices, proved to be popular. And because communities are generally very closely knit in Laos, we could address all the women in the community, not just the ones with babies. Immunisation, diarrhoea-control, early stimulation for children — we were able to combine all these into one programme. It was an integrated women's development programme that was also combined with an early childhood development programme, through the Women's Union, who were very active and supportive. They really liked the programme.

Soon after, there was an emerging development community in Laos. There were more bilateral agencies interested in working with UNICEF Laos, so we set up an Education Sector Working Group. We also had a Women's Development Working Group so that we could share and exchange ideas and information about who was doing what. At that time, there were not as many agencies, so it was quite easy to have regular meetings. These sector-specific working groups, especially the Education Sector Working Group, continue today.

From Singapore to Mongolia and Romania: Taking Early Childhood Development Further with UNICEF

Khoo Kim Choo

Dr Khoo Kim Choo is a Singaporean pioneer in the early childhood field with over 25 years of experience. She has served as a resource person and consultant to many local and international organisations, including the Singapore government, Singapore International Foundation, Save the Children, The World Bank, ASEAN,[1] UNESCO and UNICEF. She was the former Executive Director for the NTUC Childcare group and the RTRC Asia. She received the Public Service Award (PBM) from Singapore President S R Nathan in 2007 for her contribution to the field of early childhood development.

My involvement with UNICEF started in the mid-1980s and my latest encounter was in 2012. They were in different countries and in different capacities — first as a recipient of UNICEF services through their consultants to my organisation, then as collaborator, consultant and as resource person. It has taken me to Thailand, Malaysia and further afield to Mongolia, Romania and the Fiji Islands. On reflection, it has been a very satisfying relationship that has helped the early childhood field in Singapore, within the region and beyond. Encounters with UNICEF have been positive, and there are three persons from UNICEF EAPRO[2] who left an indelible mark and to whom I am most grateful: Helen Argyriades, Sheldon Shaeffer and Jim Irvine, in chronological order.

---

[1] Association of Southeast Asian Nations.
[2] UNICEF EAPRO is the UNICEF Regional Office for East Asia and the Pacific, based in Bangkok, Thailand.

UNICEF and the Beginnings of a Training Centre for Early Childhood Education

I was a fresh PhD graduate in 1983 who had done her dissertation with the National Trades Union Congress (NTUC)[3] Childcare on cognitive problem solving among four-year-old children. Immediately upon completion of my studies, I was invited to join NTUC to "train, train and train" as there was no childcare training in Singapore then. At that time, the NTUC had recently taken over the operation of all 11 childcare centres from the Ministry of Social Affairs. Services provided then were mainly custodial in nature, and the children were primarily from low-income families. I saw the situation as an opportunity for early intervention and developmental work. Children at risk could be identified early and parents could be helped to understand, manage and support their children more appropriately. Teachers needed training to understand how children learn and to move from a teacher-directed, didactic strategy to one that is more child-centred and interactive. I was enthusiastic. There was much to be done.

By sheer coincidence, it was timely that the Bernard van Leer (BvL) Foundation, from the Netherlands, was looking to fund innovative projects for disadvantaged children worldwide — and in Singapore, NTUC Childcare fitted the bill. Over 10 years the Foundation supported three projects that I directed. Together, they contributed considerably to the professional development of teachers, principals and trainers as well as the quality of childcare, not only in NTUC but also in Singapore over time.

In 1984, the first BvL project on "Upgrading Quality of Care" was to train supervisors and teachers, to develop a curriculum for different age groups and to engage parents in the centres. I needed trainers in early childhood education to help me with the training of Supervisors. As luck would have it, Helen Argyriades from UNICEF EAPRO was in town. I shared my plans and needs with her. She was interested in the training and without hesitation said she would help. And she did. She found and sponsored, not one but two trainers — one from the Hong Kong University and another from an Israeli university. They were excellent and together with my Assistant Director, we delivered the course on early childhood care, development and education. That was the first solid training in NTUC Childcare. We had converted one of the children's rooms into a modest training centre and a small room as its library. I was more concerned about the software than the hardware, the course content and process rather than the facilities.

---

[3] The National Trades Union Congress (NTUC) is a national federation of trade unions in the industrial, service and public sectors of Singapore. NTUC Childcare started off as a department of NTUC before becoming a co-operative in 1992.

This was the beginning that eventually laid the foundation for the Regional Training and Resource Centre for Early Childhood Care and Education (RTRC) Asia in 1989. It is, today, one of the largest and most established training agency in Singapore, offering training from certificated courses, diplomas to degrees and masters programmes in collaboration with Wheelock College in Boston, United States. It also offers training-of-trainers workshops to other countries within and beyond Asia. Helen Argyriades was involved as well and supported our early seminars to upgrade quality of care, development and education. Little did I realise that after her there would be further encounters with UNICEF in the years ahead.

Bringing Regional Practitioners and Experts to Singapore

A second BvL project on Parent and Community Involvement (1986–1992) took off but it was a third five-year project, the RTRC Asia (1998–2003), where UNICEF came into the picture again.

RTRC Asia was the first of three regional centres to be set up by the BvL Foundation in the following regions: Asia, Africa and the Caribbean islands. RTRC Asia's role was to support other BvL projects in Asia through training of trainers, workshops, conferences and seminars of common interest and concern. It also facilitated exchanges between and among projects from different countries as well as published and disseminated the Asian Network Newsletter to BvL projects and partners like UNICEF and Save the Children.

UNICEF was partner and co-organiser to many of RTRC's conferences. Sometimes, the UNICEF's Education Advisor, Sheldon Shaeffer, would be involved in discussion on the content and would help in identifying and sponsoring resource people as well. His contribution was very much appreciated. Save the Children was also one of RTRC's partners. Some of the institute and conference themes included "Meeting the Needs of Children in the 1990s: Prospects and Challenges" (1991); "Child Survival and Development: Parents as Catalyst" (1993); "Children of Urban Families" (1994); and "Young Children, Families and the Community: An Integrated Approach" (1997). Participants came from different Asian countries — North and South Korea, Japan, China, Malaysia, Thailand, Vietnam, Indonesia, Philippines and Cambodia. UNICEF's sponsorship made it possible for delegates from several developing countries to attend the various seminars.

These regional gatherings allowed those working with young children to share ideas to learn from one another and from experts within and outside the region — including from the United States, United Kingdom, Canada and Australia. I believe it raised the level of awareness of development in the early childhood field to the next level.

Training of Trainers: The Multiplier Effect

Training-of-trainers (TOT) workshops — on training strategies, working with parents and curriculum — were offered regularly. Such training had a multiplier effect as participants returned home to train others what they had gained — both in content and process. UNICEF country officers would identify early childhood staff who could benefit from the training and support their participation. The workshop helped to raise both knowledge and skills of trainers and potential trainers. I often associate the appearance of Jim Irvine, who came after Sheldon, with the TOT. Jim was the new Regional Education Advisor.

When the BvL Foundation decided to change strategy and stopped working through RTRC after five years, we were determined to continue with the TOT programme. Faced with no further funding for TOT workshops, Jim Irvine and I discussed the possibility of support from the Ministry of Foreign Affairs' (MFA) Technical Co-operation Directorate. Jim met with MFA and we were delighted at the final outcome. A tripartite arrangement was agreed upon whereby RTRC would offer the training, UNICEF would identify and sponsor trainees' travel costs from different countries to Singapore and MFA would sponsor trainees' accommodation costs when in Singapore and pay for the training by RTRC. I was pleased that this was settled before I left NTUC and RTRC Asia. Under this new arrangement, the TOT workshop started in 1999 and except for 2013 and 2014, have continued to this day. Now, countries as far away as Africa, the Middle East and Eastern Europe come for the training as well. RTRC Asia has since been renamed SEED Institute.

Those were hectic but exciting times and an example of where a project has extended into an ongoing programme that served not only those in the early childhood field in Singapore but so many other countries in the developing world as well.

A New Role: Consulting for UNICEF

In 1998, I was invited by Save the Children (UK) and UNICEF Mongolia, to undertake a mission for Mongolia's Ministry of Science, Technology, Education and Culture (MOSTEC). Earlier official visits to Mongolia for meetings and training had given me some background on the country. This mission was to review and recommend development and upgrading of the Teachers Training College for the implementation of the National Preschool Education Programme and to follow up with some of the 20 Mongolian participants who had attended the TOT in Singapore. UNICEF had special interest in reaching out to children of poor nomadic families. The mission had to be completed within five working days. So it was a flurry of meetings with key people in the MOSTEC, Teacher Training College, and visits to secondary and primary schools and some kindergartens in the urban and rural areas. There were also meetings with institutions, instructors, teachers and parents, UNICEF, Save the Children and joint meetings with major agencies involved in the National Preschool Planning. The meetings, by and large, went well and I did not feel there was any resistance to suggestions.

Mongolian participants who attended RTRC TOT were observed to be able to implement what they had learnt — judging by the classroom environment, their teaching and the response from the children and trainees. The teachers and trainers were more interactive and used different strategies while the children and trainees were more vocal and participative. This was a change from the usual didactic, teacher-directed style. These new skills and knowledge had to be disseminated to other teachers and trainers.

With regard to nomadic families, the children received scattered and sporadic exposure to early childhood education. Kindergarten teachers might visit the family for a week to a month. Sometimes parents would send their children to a kindergarten when they visited the town. There were also schools with dormitories that offered kindergarten lessons for a month before the children started formal schooling. For these families, a child-to-child programme where an older sibling taught a young one through play and games would be helpful in facilitating development. And since Mongolia had a fairly high literacy rate, parents could pick up material and resources made by the Resource Centre when they were in town to use with their young children.

As Mongolia was turning into a market economy, many changes were quickly taking place with the influx of mass media influence and foreign values. Privatisation of some state services had, in the case of kindergartens, deprived poor children of an early childhood education. Some NGOs had stepped in to help. Mongolian children would face a very different future where they needed a second language, possibly English, to interact with the outside world. Suggestions to MOSTEC related to the duration of the teacher training course, training in Singapore and Mongolia, the national preschool curriculum, and building of early childhood resources for trainers and teachers.

After Mongolia, I was involved with Phase 1 of an ASEAN project in 1999. ASEAN member countries, having earlier agreed to collaborate on a five-year project on early child care and development, held their first Experts Group Meeting (EGM) in Singapore with UNICEF sponsorship. Jim Irvine, UNICEF's Regional Education Advisor, played a significant role in this meeting. He presented an integrated UNICEF perspective on early childhood care for survival, growth and development, UNICEF's priorities and goals for 2000–2005, as well as some recommendations for members' consideration. I was there to assist UNICEF prepare and plan for the Experts Group Meeting and a subsequent UNICEF-Singapore TOT that same year. My role was also to present childcare options and training issues to the meeting.

It was a good beginning for ASEAN countries to discuss the status of early childhood care and development in their own countries, identify common gaps and needs and have discussion groups on programme and policy, curriculum and training and system of licensing and monitoring. The common trend of more women joining the labour force and the decline of the extended family contributed to the increasing need for alternative childcare arrangements. Although different countries faced different struggles and challenges — poverty, social and economic turmoil following the 1997 economic crises and competing needs for resources — there was an expressed commitment from all ASEAN countries to work towards the care, development and education of all children. The desired outcome would be to develop a comprehensive and integrated system for all young children that would be sustainable in the long run. Sharing resources and expertise would be a good start to expedite changes and avoid re-inventing the wheel. The cooperation is reflected by different countries volunteering to be responsible for different areas to benefit the group. This ranged from compilation of a directory of training, resource persons and other related resources, to a directory of programmes in ASEAN countries; development of minimum standards, licensing and monitoring, and developmentally appropriate early childhood care and education curricula; creation of training programme for early childhood practitioners; strengthening of a regional network; and development of a framework for a comprehensive perspective of early childhood for ASEAN countries. All these recommendations were to be prepared for the second phase of the ASEAN project that was to take place in the Philippines in 2000.

After the ASEAN consultancy, one of the rather interesting consultancies that took me further afield was in Romania in July 2000. I was to join a team of three Romanian consultants to assess UNICEF's five-year National Family Education Programme that had two components: a formal education component including the early childhood programme, training of social workers, nurses and teachers, and an informal education component on parent education, community development (especially in the Roma community) and education for the prevention of HIV/Aids. It was an ambitious coverage. Furthermore, at the last minute, the other international consultant who was supposed to lead the team was unable to make it and I was tasked to lead the team instead. That was quite a challenge.

The work required considerable travelling from Bucharest in the south to the east, central, west and north of Romania. We visited and spoke to communities, including the Roma community and their home-based preschool. It was interesting to note that although a new state kindergarten was available for the Roma children along the main road, hardly any attended that kindergarten. Instead, the community, away from the main road, had set up its own home-based kindergarten that I visited. One possible reason could be that the new kindergarten was mainstream and the community felt that it did not reflect their values and culture as well as their language. The Roma were friendly and at the same time, amused and curious to see me — perhaps because for many I was the first Chinese person they had met. The team also visited orphanages and state institutions for young children. Institutional care by the state was once deemed desirable for their "proper" care, development and education. At the time of this consultancy, there was a move by the state to de-institutionalise children and return them to their families. This move from state to family would require some transitional support to help parents to assume responsibility for their own children's care and development once again.

I remember being on the road for quite a bit as we traversed through the beautiful countryside and seeing "Dracula's castle" along the way. Romania was going through political and social changes at that time.

At the office, I met with the UNICEF Chief and the Education Advisor to discuss the project, my impression of the services, and the programmes. A final report consolidating the recommendations from the team of consultants was submitted when I was back in Singapore. The rest was up to the local consultants to follow through.

My last experience with UNICEF was through the Asia-Pacific Regional Network for Early Childhood (ARNEC), a UNICEF-UNESCO initiative that was moved from Bangkok to Singapore. I was involved on the periphery, engaging in informal sharing and moderating one of their conference sessions.[4] ARNEC's work includes supporting and collaborating with early childhood projects in Asia-Pacific countries. When the Pacific Early Childhood Care and Education Council was formed and its 1st Meeting was held in 2012, I was one of the resource persons there at the invitation of ARNEC and UNICEF Fiji, to present Singapore's guidelines and framework for 0 to 6 year olds. The Fiji situation was unique to me because of the geographical make-up of so many small islands — beautiful but fragmented — that pose challenges to the early childhood community. Early childhood leaders travel by boat or small aircraft to visit

---

[4] ARNEC was the result of a Joint UNICEF-UNESCO Early Childhood Policy Review Project (2006–2008).

the early childhood centres located on small islands. It reflects a commitment to children, no matter how difficult the circumstances. In spite of the challenges, the leaders were determined to collectively work towards better and sustainable policies, systems, operations and quality starting from the bottom up. The formation and work of the Council was, indeed, commendable with the full support from UNICEF behind it.

Conclusion

My work with UNICEF has brought me varied experiences — both challenging and intriguing. At all times, I have found working with various UNICEF personnel, mainly Education Advisors, pleasant in all instances, and memorable in some cases. Although I cannot remember all their names, I remember their faces, their deep concern for disadvantaged children and families and their attempts to improve their lives. For early childhood specialists who seek to work with young children and families in various difficult circumstances beyond Singapore, UNICEF would offer such an experience. If there are opportunities to engage UNICEF, as RTRC Asia had done and is still doing, I would urge Singaporeans to explore the possibility of doing so.

My thanks to UNICEF for the journey and I hope the Singapore-UNICEF partnership will continue to improve the lives of disadvantaged children and families beyond the shores of Singapore.

From Italy to Vietnam:
Two Very Different UNICEF Operations

Peggy Kek

Peggy Kek is a Singaporean who worked with UNICEF as Assistant Fundraising Officer and consultant from 1991 to 1995, in Singapore, Vietnam and China. Here she recounts how visits to two very different operations, early in her career, provided her with useful information and invaluable insights into the workings of UNICEF.

The majority of UNICEF's offices are located in developing countries in Asia, Africa and Latin America. Only headquarters, regional offices and specialised offices are located in developed cities such as New York, Geneva, Copenhagen (which is the logistics and supplies hub) and Singapore (which was a production centre for the Greeting Card Operation, or GCO).

In 1993 and 1994, I had the opportunity to leave my Singapore base and interact with two very different aspects of UNICEF work on opposite sides of the world in Italy and Vietnam. The visits gave me invaluable insights into the complexity of UNICEF's mandate and the distinct purviews of different offices that support it.

An Insight into Italy's Special Contributions One Year

In industrialised countries that no longer receive assistance from UNICEF, the government and other institutions sometimes cooperate with UNICEF for the benefit of the countries that still require assistance. This may be in the form of financial contributions to specific assistance programmes, other times it could be the sharing of experience and knowledge. In 2009, for instance, I worked with the Singapore Ministry of Foreign Affairs and the Lee Kuan Yew School of Public

Policy at the National University of Singapore to organise a regional conference on the "Impact of the Economic Crisis on Children". Conceptualised by Dr Mahesh Patel, then UNICEF Regional Adviser for Social Policy and Economic Analysis, the conference provided an important platform for participants to learn from one another about the fiscal challenges posed by the 2008 global financial crisis and the threats that budgetary cuts could have on the well-being of children.

In other countries such as the United States of America, Canada, Japan and most countries in Western Europe, National Committees for UNICEF have been set up to raise awareness and funds for UNICEF's programmes in developing countries. By chance one year, I got to know more about the work of the Italian Committee.

UNICEF cards over the years had come to be known for the use of art from prestigious museums and renowned artists. People around the world are known to buy UNICEF cards not just to support children, but also to collect the artworks. For artists, to have an artwork selected for a UNICEF card is also regarded as a badge of honour. UNICEF staff and National Committees would submit suggestions from around the globe and GCO would convene an annual meeting to select the designs for each year. In 1993, the meeting was organised in the Tuscan city of Florence, with the help of the Italian Committee for UNICEF.

The Committee was founded in 1974 to advocate for children's rights and raise funds to support UNICEF programmes in developing countries. It has more than 100 sub-committees managed by volunteers and a professional staff based in Rome. Its awareness-raising campaigns involve a wide number of stakeholders from citizens to mayors and local authorities, schools and universities, companies and NGO partners, Goodwill Ambassadors, the media and the government.

UNICEF's strong presence in Italy was one reason that Florence was a fitting venue for the meeting. Also, while UNICEF produced cards for many religious holidays, Christmas cards were by far the bestsellers, and Italian museums gave generously of their many Christian religious artworks for UNICEF's use. When it was time to have a meeting that year, the venerable Uffizi museum in Florence offered its historical premises for the meeting. I happened to be in Italy that year on a personal visit and attended the meeting as an observer. As someone who would be promoting the sale of the cards a year later in Singapore, it was fascinating to watch and hear the marketing and artistic considerations that went into making the choices for that year's card collection.

I took the opportunity to visit the then-called UNICEF International Child Development Centre in Florence. Opened in 1988 the centre was established to identify and research current and future areas of UNICEF work. While it has since been renamed the UNICEF-Innocenti Office of Research, its objectives have remained unchanged — "to improve international understanding of issues relating to children's rights, and to help facilitate full implementation of the Convention on the Rights of the Child supporting advocacy worldwide." The Centre was hosted by the Italian government in the 600-year-old premises of a former hospital for children, the Ospedale degli Innocenti. It was an example of how UNICEF depended on gifts of different kinds to carry out its mandate.

A Glimpse of Vietnam Two Decades Ago

The following year in 1994, the Singapore office took on the role of advising certain Country Offices in the region on how to introduce marketing strategies for the sale of cards and gifts. The growing success of what we had managed to do in Singapore and other countries had caught the attention of some of these other offices. I went to share our experiences and to carry out market research to help map out strategies to do the same in Vietnam in 1994 and China in 1995.

During that first visit to Vietnam in 1994, I was struck and shocked by the number of disabled people in the streets. Some, with one leg, stood at traffic junctions on crutches, begging. Others without both legs, would lie on crudely assembled, flat wooden boards fitted with wheels, and push themselves along pavements. Many of them were victims of anti-personnel landmines.

The use of anti-personnel landmines was an issue that was emerging in the early 1990s and which eventually gained greater salience in the late 1990s when British Princess Diana's involvement drew more media attention to it.

These were cruel weapons that continued to maim and kill even after a war was over. The mines could be and were mistaken for toys by children. Landmines also cause huge swathes of arable land to become unusable. Removing the landmines in order to render the land available to farmers again was high-cost and high-risk.

During my assignment, I had the opportunity to travel with the UNICEF Vietnam communications team to see some of the projects that UNICEF had supported. In one village in a rural province in the north of Vietnam, I saw papaya trees planted all along the main road to encourage mothers to give to their children the easily available local fruit which was a rich source of vitamins and minerals. On market day, in the village centre, women would sing songs containing health messages about certain important nutrients or HIV-AIDS transmission. I learnt from my colleagues that these creative and simple approaches to advocacy were also very effective.

We stayed in the village that night. As we were checking into a small guest-house, I spotted a couple of rats scurrying around in the small reception area. Terrified that the rats would make their way into my room, I did not sleep that night. The next day we continued our journey in the four-wheel drive jeep. We went over long stretches of bumpy dirt roads and narrow paths between padi fields, eventually arriving at a remote hilltop with a wonderful view of the mountainous surroundings.

There, in a rudimentary one-room cement building was a school. The school was the result of a partnership between UNICEF and Save the Children as well as the people of the village, who built the school themselves with the cement that was bought for them.

As we sat there observing the class, about six chickens clucked away outside in the schoolyard and one or two even occasionally hopped nonchalantly into the classroom. They were part of a deceptively modest but innovative and effective way of overcoming the difficulty of attracting teachers to the remotely located school. The additional income from selling the eggs in the market went into supplementing the low salaries of the teachers. Unsold eggs were given to the more malnourished children, providing a precious source of protein and calories. Nothing was wasted, everything was cherished.

Back in Singapore

Back in Singapore, I felt that personally seeing the two different UNICEF operations in Italy and Vietnam had helped me to be better at my job because I could be a more convincing communicator, and hence better advocate for children. Both the visits to Italy and Vietnam were eye-opening and each inspired in its own way. For me it was very informative to see how widespread the support for UNICEF was throughout Italy — in government, businesses, NGOs, schools and museums. And in Vietnam I saw for the first time, a beneficiary of UNICEF's programmes. Seeing the children, with their blue school bags and exercise books with the UNICEF logo on them, seated at the wooden desks in the school on that remote hilltop, really brought home to me why we did what we did in the UNICEF Singapore office.

The Power of a Little Trust and Credit

Ng Shui-Meng with Peggy Kek[1]

Dr Ng Shui-Meng worked in UNICEF China's Social Development Programme for Poor Areas (SPPA) from 1996 to 2000. While the Eastern coastal areas of China were rapidly growing in wealth, the inner provinces, particularly in the West of China lagged in both economic opportunities and social conditions. She was asked to work on a community-level project targeting women. The use of microfinance in development was beginning to gain traction. UNICEF devised the programme using micro-credit to build up the women's economic capacity in order to improve the lives of their children.

When I was working in China on the Social Development Programme for Poor Areas (SPPA), I spent a lot of time travelling to different parts of the enormous country, into its depths and heartlands where most foreigners, at that time, did not visit.

We designed a programme using microfinance to reach poor women. We selected 24 poor counties. They were all in the West — in Inner Mongolia, Xinjiang, Tibet, Gansu, Guizhou, Yunnan and Guangxi.

We had specific criteria that the women had to fulfil. In order to participate in the programme, the women had to make certain commitments. There were eight commitments, all relating to improving the health and education status of children. And all focused on the women's knowledge of breastfeeding, use of iodised salt, immunisation of children, sending their children to school, health practices and so on. One was a health and sanitation requirement: you had to build a toilet. In China, improving sanitation was one of the biggest challenges.

---

[1] This account is based on an interview by Peggy Kek on 6 June 2015.

The loans were for their own income generation. In those days, many households were looking for ways to improve their own production. It was during the time that ideas about the market economy were flourishing in Eastern China. In the Western parts, it wasn't that the people had no ideas, but they had no access to capital and the banks were not responding.

We were very successful in convincing the local governments that it was good to target women, that they were loan-worthy even without collateral. We used the system of mutual monitoring, same as in the Grameen Bank in Bangladesh. The borrowers had to organise group meetings, attend the meetings, encourage one another, repay the loans through monthly payments, and build up savings. After the loans were repaid, they could get another loan.

Each loan amount was about RMB 1,000 and they had to have a business plan, they had to report on it, they had to repay it. The repayment interest rate was about 20%. It was decided not by UNICEF but by a consultative process. If the households were to borrow from a local moneylender, the interest would have been 40%. So our interest rate was agreed at 20%, half of that.

Many of the women were very enterprising. Some of them were in need of just a little bit of capital to expand the cotton production, in the case of poor households in Xinjiang, or to raise more ducks or geese, so that they could sell the down. They were all small enterprises — setting up small shops and small eateries such as noodle shops. The women were looking for opportunities to expand their production — some of them to expand, some to start. We monitored their ability to grow their business and also their actual impact on their households. We were more interested in how they were impacting their households, and how they were honouring their commitments vis-à-vis children.

We found the programme was especially useful in areas such as Inner Mongolia where it's a pastoral community and the women had to ride on a horse for an hour to get to the meeting place! For some of the women, where it was still very conservative, they were not supposed to go and "chit-chat" with the neighbours because it was thought, "There is so much work to do. You're poor, why are you wasting time gossiping?" And so on.

But one of the conditions of the loan was that they had to attend the meetings. So the monthly meeting provided them with a legitimate reason to get together and have some social interaction for one or two hours. Each meeting had a group of about 15 to 20 women.

Apart from repaying their loans, there was a whole curriculum they had to go through. The local person responsible for the project would speak on issues like the value of good hygiene practices, exclusive breastfeeding, supplementary feeding, use of iodised salt and immunisation. They would have someone to lead the meeting. And they had to develop a meeting programme.

It was a collective. They were responsible for one another's loans. That gave them an incentive to come to the meeting. "What happens if a member of my group doesn't come to the meeting?" It was a kind of a group guarantee, with a very strong dynamic. It really worked.

I remember in Heilongjiang one year, there was a flood. We went to do the monitoring and the counties insisted that the women had to repay their loans. We told them no, they had to understand the conditions and why the borrowers couldn't pay up. Their ducks were all gone. So we told them to give these women more time. We told them UNICEF was not about collecting debt. It was also about learning. And you don't want to drive these women to desperation. So there's some debt forgiving.

At the local level, there was the whole process of learning how to deal with debt and how to deal with emergency — to have some social protection system that must kick in during an emergency.

UNICEF piloted the programme, to be taken over by the county governments, if it proved successful. Once we had shown them how to do it and it was demonstrated to work, many county governments said they would take over. They used the local banks and banking system.

We showed the counties that it was worthwhile — trusting the women and that they were credit-worthy. The assessment quite interestingly showed that one of the spillover effects was that for the women in these very poor areas who did not have many opportunities to get together, the monthly meetings were an opportunity for them to gather together, exchange ideas not just about doing small businesses, but also to compare social information.

The programme was very successful.[2] In fact, TVE made a documentary about it, called *Because They're Worth It*.[3] In the film, one of the women described what UNICEF had helped achieve through the programme, in a few simple lines: "Diet. Sanitation. Health. Everything has changed."

---

[2] Coincidentally, Singaporean Cheng Wing-Sie, also a contributor to this volume, was one of the evaluators of the programme.

[3] TVE is a not-for-profit that works with filmmakers and partners worldwide to make and distribute films that put the environment and sustainability on the global agenda. The documentary can be viewed at http://tve.org/film/life-because-theyre-worth-it/.

"Chatting With My Best Friend": Fighting HIV-AIDS in Nepal

Cheng Wing-Sie with Peggy Kek[1]

Cheng Wing-Sie was Chief of Communication for the UNICEF Nepal office from 1999 to 2002. At the time, there was a surge in HIV infections among youth in high-risk groups; of about 30,000 cases of HIV/AIDS in Nepal in 1998, nearly half were people aged between 15 and 25. She was asked to come up with a communication strategy to help counter the trend. This is the story of the phenomenal success of Saathi Sanga Munka Kura, or "Chatting with My Best Friend", a radio programme that UNICEF launched as part of the strategy.

In 1999, UNICEF created a radio programme called "Chatting with My Best Friend". It was the first such programme in Nepal — run by young people — for young people. When I moved to Kathmandu that same year, the Nepal office made HIV a focal point and I started to wonder what had happened to the epidemic. From my initial observation, Nepal's epidemic was not so much fuelled by sex but through the injection of drugs.

Globally, there was an emerging approach to preventing drug use. Called "life skills education", it focused on cultivating inner resilience. So I thought, here's the chance to translate this into edutainment, which was a huge task. UNICEF did a round of consultations with the partners in Nepal on what vital intervention they thought was missing. They all pointed to communication — and they were looking to UNICEF for this, to target teenagers and young people. And I had a

[1] This account is based on an interview by Peggy Kek on 29 April 2015.

very fulfilling time working on this Communication for Development (C4D)[2] initiative.

When we conducted the focus groups and surveys, we realised that teenagers, adolescents, as a notion, did not even exist in the Nepali lexicon. For the Nepalese, children leapt from childhood to adulthood. The concept of adolescence with specific needs, puberty and all, did not exist. So when we talked to parents, they all told us the same thing — children, they would grow up by themselves, from being babies to being ready for marriage. They knew little about adolescence.

At the time, HIV was clearly a young person's issue in Nepal, especially when you look at the age and the data, where quite a number started to take drugs when they were young. It starts with a lot of gateway behaviour: they start with pain-killers, easily available across the border from India, and then they get into heroin and injections, and that's how HIV gets passed on.

At that time, life skills education was the one approach being promoted widely. We had established that radio was the most accessible communications means that reached out to all corners of Nepal. I gathered the UNICEF team and brought in consultants to create a year-long series of radio programmes: a chat show for young people, run by young people. It was all in Nepali. I didn't know a word of Nepali and had to rely on translations. So I worked with translators and focused on the concept and providing the leadership.

When it first went on air, my goodness, even Sherpas in the mountains said that they had tuned in to the programme! Eventually it reached young people in China's Tibet Autonomous Region, in the states of Uttar Pradesh and Bihar in northern India, and in Bhutan.

This was the approach we adopted: Encouraging the two young hosts to invite listeners to write in to share their issues. Because they were to be the listeners' best friend — hence the show's title "Chatting with My Best Friend" — I told the young producers that there was only one standard they needed to follow for the programme, and it could not be compromised: They really had to make themselves their listeners' best friend. Think back to what they would say to their best friend, what they would do for their best friend. Be their best friend.

---

[2] C4D is communicating beyond just giving information. It involves understanding people's beliefs and values, and their social and cultural norms. It involves engaging communities and listening to how they identify the problems and propose solutions. C4D uses a range of communication tools and approaches that empower individuals and communities to take actions to improve their lives. For more formation on C4D, visit http://www.unicef.org/cbsc.

We received overwhelming feedback — sometimes as many as 200 letters a day, up to 700 letters a week. Some teenagers would walk two hours to a post box to mail their letters. That radio programme generated a groundswell of support among listeners.

Within six months, 700 listener clubs were set up all over Nepal. It addressed an immense hunger for knowledge related to sexual reproductive health, boy-girl relationships and more ("he jilted me", "she doesn't want to talk to me", "how do I deal with parental pressures"). When we sat down to analyse those letters, we could categorise them into a number of issues — mostly revolving around relationships — with peers, with siblings and with parents.

The hosts were four young Nepalis. They took turns; a boy and a girl each time. Guiding them was a gifted Harvard graduate who was a UNICEF consultant we had, who helped translate the listeners' issues and linked them to the 10 life skills we were promoting. It is a very interesting concept developed from Cornell University in the United States, and I used that and translated it into edutainment for the programme.

Foremost, these skills were self-awareness; responsible decision-making and making responsible choices; creative thinking; communications skills; critical thinking (critical thinking is particularly important, so that when one is under peer pressure, one can discern whether it's good or bad); how to creatively communicate one's fears; and how to get in touch with one's emotions and feelings. All these also require one to become more aware.

Life skills education was a recognised intervention in UNICEF at that time, but Nepal was really the first nation outside of Sub-Saharan Africa that translated it into an edutainment package. We used these letters as examples and inspiration for stories. We weaved life skills into these stories, into these dramas, and got a bunch of young people to perform these dramas on the radio programme. The radio show subsequently had a spin-off TV soap opera.

It was truly something very satisfying. Every day when the office messenger brought in stacks of letters — that really made our day. Even my boss would tell the office, "Every field trip I went on, as soon as I said I'm from UNICEF, they would say 'Saathi, Saathi....'" (The Nepali name for the programme is *Saathi Sanga Manka Kura*, or "My Friend Who Knows My Heart".) He said, "Never in my 30-year career in UNICEF have I encountered anything as popular as this." Every village we went, there was that recognition of UNICEF and *Saathi Sanga Manka Kura*. Those stacks of letters were really amazing.

Also, with teenagers, one really cannot be too sanitised. We had to get into issues without feeling too squeamish. For instance, as many as 500 letters came from boys saying that their penis was too short, and that it affected their self-confidence. And girls would ask about menstruation. We had so many issues surrounding sexual reproductive health that were taboo — and this was where the programme tried to educate, in an entertaining way.

We had to answer these questions — and answer them directly. For instance, other than a blood-borne disease, HIV is also sexually transmitted. We had to look at these issues holistically, and as science, even though in a traditional, conservative society like Nepal, it was not easy.

We did manage to sneak in one programme, an episode about addressing sexual desires. The Director-General of radio, as soon as Monday came (the programme was transmitted every Saturday) called and told us to be careful, and not to talk about these things on air. "No, no sex on air." I told my boss I was expecting it, and replied reassuringly, "Don't worry, the next few weeks we'll only talk about Vitamin A and immunisation — no sex!"

I found the work very satisfying during this period, analysing those letters that came in, categorising them and creating pie charts as the basis to plan future episodes. I was truly heartened when one teenager wrote in and said: "Thanks to your programme, my brother decided to quit drugs. You saved his life."

Meant to be a year-long radio series when when it was first planned, "Chatting with My Best Friend" has been running for 16 years now. It has won three international awards and has become an institution in Nepal. It accompanied the growth of a generation of Nepali children, and helped youth feel a little less alone grappling with insecurities and the many challenges of growing up, figuring out who they are. That's what made me really proud. It is so relevant.

Emergency Mode in Timor-Leste

Ng Shui-Meng with Peggy Kek[1]

In 2004, Singaporean Dr Ng Shui-Meng was appointed UNICEF Representative in Timor-Leste. Shortly after she arrived in the newly established nation that was just recovering from decades of war, violence broke out. This was her last UNICEF position before she retired in 2008, and here she talks about the most difficult posting in her career with UNICEF.

Timor-Leste was obviously devastated, even though it was supposed to be already quite stable by the time I arrived in 2004. There was a stable government but they had to rebuild everything anew — a Ministry of Health, a Ministry of Education, etc. — and there was still peacekeeping work to be done. The United Nations Integrated Mission in Timor-Leste was still on the ground, although it was supposed to be winding down and the peacekeepers were expected to leave.

For the first year and a half, we were developing. We were helping the government to rebuild the entire education system and trying to get the Ministry to look at the curriculum. There were also bilateral partners, like the Portuguese government, who wanted to support the development. UNICEF was very well trusted by the other partners so they always consulted UNICEF and we always tried to help them. We tried to rebuild the immunisation systems. We worked very closely with the World Health Organization, with the legal sector and the Ministry of Law.

---

[1] This account is based on an interview by Peggy Kek on 6 June 2015.

But violence broke out again in 2006. This time, it was communal violence. People were burning cars and houses. The army was fighting against the police.

The UN compound was sort of sandwiched between the military headquarters on one side and the police headquarters on the other. A bullet landed in my office. Buildings in the UN compound were rather flimsy and the bullet went right through. I was walking out of my office when the bullet shot through and lodged in the wall.

We were in emergency mode. We had to evacuate the staff, leaving only the essential staff— meaning myself, the Communications Officer and the Operations Officer. Everybody else had to leave. We had to stay in the office for a few nights. We couldn't go home. It wasn't safe. And there was no food in the compound. It was quite an experience.

Some of my local staff were calling me on the phone, "Oh people are shooting, attacking my house, what am I to do?" We had to think about protecting the staff. We had to think about we had to do. For the first 24 hours, there were so many emergency meetings. Different agencies became responsible for different things. The UN compound was almost like a military strategic planning and control centre.

There were many internally displaced persons — people who had lost their homes or had nowhere to go but were not quite legally recognised as refugees. There were camps set up just outside the UN compound. I remember on the third or fourth day after the camps were set up, somebody came in shouting, "Someone's going to deliver a baby!" And we had nothing.

One of the best things to emerge from the emergency programme was that all the agencies came closer together. In peace time there may be agency egos, personality egos and so on. But in emergency time, all that goes out of the window. Everybody just came together and focused on the essentials. Where were our resources, where could we focus? Where were our competencies? And it just made sense for all of us to go back to our bread and butter areas.

UNICEF took the lead in immunisation, child protection, providing safe spaces for children and education. Although we usually had a big role in water and sanitation, during the emergency OXFAM took the lead and we supported them. UNHCR[2] had the tents, the housing; and World Food Programme had the food, which was badly needed by the displaced. And we had regular meetings of all the agencies to see what we could do together or help each other.

---

[2] United Nations High Commissioner for Refugees.

Since we had evacuated all the staff, we had to seek assistance from the regional office.[3] The office had an emergency team. Some of them came from New York, some were already in place in Bangkok and they flew in to help. The Regional Director then was Anupama Rao Singh.

We also had frequent conference calls with our headquarters in New York, either very early or very late at the end of day, to report back. The purpose was to find out what we needed. They were trying to mobilise resources for us as quickly as possible, to get resources to the ground. We needed to fly in things — health packs, School in a Box, water and sanitation supplies, and more.

During the emergency, in the first few months, we focused on preventing disease outbreak, on making sure that we had vaccination for polio in all the camps. We had safe places for children, for protection, so that there would be no abuse of children, and no gender abuse. We made sure that the latrines were well located — for males and for females — and trained a lot of people. We provided a lot of child protection technical support to the Ministry of Social Welfare.

We were also starting programmes for young people. There were so many young people. Much of the violence was being carried out by the young and unemployed. They got into fights in one camp, got drunk in another, and so on. We worked on getting them to be more engaged in doing something useful. The United Nations Development Programme (UNDP) had a work programme and we focused on that. We got the youth to work with UNDP, to volunteer to clean the streets.

It was a very intense period. We were so tired, so exhausted. Every morning, there would be a team meeting on what we were doing, on what had happened in the camps, reporting back on where we should be diverting most of our resources and where we should assign our staff — to the camp that needed us most.

We worked also with the local groups, the convents, the church groups. By giving them the resources, they could do their work.

We also had to work with the peacekeepers. We had to make sure that the peacekeepers understood issues related to child rights because they were guarding the camps. The situation in an emergency or war-torn place can be very precarious. The peacekeepers themselves can sometimes be the violators. So we had to work very closely with the SRSG[4] and with the peacekeeping forces.

---

[3] Timor-Leste came under UNICEF's East Asia and Pacific Regional Office (also known as EAPRO), located in Bangkok.

[4] Special Representative of the Secretary-General of the United Nations.

We were running workshops on child rights issues, on how to watch out for abuses, how to make sure that the children are not in a vulnerable position. We had to put in a reporting system and got the Ministry to put welfare workers in the camps to watch out for possible abuses. It was not easy.

And then there were so many people coming in to help. I remember there was this group of volunteers from Singapore. They were all very well-intentioned but they were trying to distribute breast milk substitutes[5] because they said the children needed milk powder. So we said no, they could not distribute milk powder. We were trying to get them to understand, that for them, it was about giving, it was a welfare issue, but there were other consequences. They said, "But it's written on the pack that it shouldn't be given to children under three." We explained, "Everybody is hungry. If this packet of milk goes into a family and they have children from 0 to 5 years old, all of them are going to be drinking from the pack. How are you going to ensure that the babies are not given the milk? Also, given the unsanitary conditions of the water in the camp, babies fed on milk made from milk powder would be at risk of getting diarrhoea."

At the same time, the press were after us for information on who was doing what. The point is, there were a lot of people coming in; that made managing the emergency, the media and the volunteers very intense.

It was the most difficult posting I had. You always had to be on the alert. And sometimes you had to make decisions on the spot — about what, where and who. You also had to deal a lot with staff issues. Some of them couldn't go home. I had two staff whom I allowed to sleep in the office. It was not permitted, but what could I do? Push them out? They had no homes to go back to.

It was a difficult posting in terms of making sure the staff were safe, especially the Timorese staff, and also making sure that the programme was still addressing the needs.

Among staff, about one-third were international and two-thirds local. The latter were mostly drivers, project assistants, secretaries and supplies staff. International staff mostly worked in health, education and protection. There were also UN volunteers and other volunteers, as well as consultants who came in. For me, the backbone was really the Timorese staff. I felt that if the Timorese staff felt safe, if they felt that their welfare was being taken care of, if they felt that you cared for them, then they were much more committed to give their best to UNICEF. So for me, it was important to give them information because there were so many rumours flying around. I had to make sure that the staff, both local and

---

[5] UNICEF advocates exclusive breastfeeding for children at least for the first six months.

international, had the same information. Whenever I had meetings to report back on what was happening, I did not have separate meetings. Everybody was in one meeting — from the Deputy Representative to the driver. This was important and helped build trust between the local and international staff.

Even during the Emergency, once things had quietened down after the first few months, we went back to supporting the original areas of work we had done before the Emergency — in education and immunisation. We operated in emergency mode for about six months, and then went back to programme work.

There was still a lot of reconstruction of communities and we were trying to get people to move back. By the time I left in 2008, there were still internally displaced persons, but the situation had calmed down significantly.

Section 2

UNICEF Internationals in Action:
UNICEF in Singapore

Singapore Impressions

Karsten Sohns

Karsten Sohns was the head of the UNICEF Greeting Card Operation (GCO) Office in Singapore from February 1988 to July 1991. He led a team of three persons to provide UNICEF greeting cards, gifts and related publicity materials to 20 UNICEF offices in Asia and the Pacific; and in Singapore to promote UNICEF card and gift sales and raise awareness. In this piece he shares his experience of his assignments for UNICEF in Brazil and Singapore and how these two centres improved flexibility and efficiency and lowered costs.

Arriving at Changi Airport Singapore from Brazil with my wife Stella and our four kids was like entering a kind of paradise. Everything seemed to be well organised, clean, efficient — even the air-conditioning worked! However, leaving the airport through the exit door was a shock as the humid, tropical heat in the middle of the day almost took our breath away.

My first thought: How was I to survive and work in such a humid heat?

I had joined UNICEF in September 1983. Prior to that I worked as a printing engineer for a commercial company in Santiago, Chile and needed to find a more suitable job in South America quickly or return with my family to Germany.

In a trade magazine I found a job advertisement from the UNICEF Greeting Card Operation (GCO) in New York for a printing expert to start the local production and distribution of UNICEF greeting cards and other products for Brazil. The goal was to de-centralise the production and distribution of the greeting cards and other products from the UNICEF Headquarters in New York to two regions — South America and Asia — to gain more flexibility, faster supplies during sales campaigns and lower costs compared to producing and shipping the items from New York as was the practice of the time.

The main objectives of UNICEF GCO worldwide were to increase awareness in the private sector of the organisation and its programmes for children in developing countries and to raise additional funds for those programmes through the sales of greeting cards and other products.

I warmed to the idea of working for an international and humanitarian organisation, applied and got the job. After three months of briefing and training in New York that included the United Nations Rules and Regulations governing procurement, operations and quality standards, we moved to Rio. At about the same time I went to Brazil to set up the Centre for South America, a colleague from the UNICEF office in New York went to Singapore to set up the Centre for Asia and the Pacific.

I became responsible for the production, storage and distribution of UNICEF greeting cards and other products for South America and for the marketing and sales in Brazil. I managed 25 staff members in three offices in Rio, Sao Paulo and Fortaleza. At that time in Brazil, there were good professional printing companies, especially in Sao Paulo, though they had less experience with the export market with the result that quality standards were not always kept as consistent as desired. Importing items and exporting greeting cards to the region often took many weeks and man-hours; and the associated costs to accomplish this could be significant.

One of the main reasons for selecting Singapore for such a centre in Asia was the reputation of its highly developed quality printing industry that was internationally competitive, thanks to its thriving export markets in Europe, the United States and Japan. Another reason was cost. Before arriving in Singapore I had met a Dutch printer who travelled regularly to Singapore to ensure quality control for colour separations, printing and binding for large print runs that were less costly for the same quality as production in Europe even after the costs of transport and additional travelling were included.

A third reason was the robust infrastructure and efficient administration that ensured that imports and exports were cleared within two to three days. This could not be matched in Bangkok, another strong candidate for the Centre and the seat of the UNICEF East Asia and Pacific Regional Office.

The United Nations has a policy of rotating staff after a given number of years in a duty station. When I became eligible, I applied successfully and became head of the UNICEF GCO office in Singapore in 1988.

In addition to myself there was a professional quality control officer, an administration clerk and an assistant clerk with experience in the warehousing and distribution sector, all Singaporeans and strongly committed to UNICEF and helping children. Even after so many years, I am still very thankful for their commitment and tremendous work.

Our work consisted mainly of securing and controlling the very best services and lowest costs available in quality print production, warehousing and distribution in Singapore. Occasionally, colleagues in the region would also ask us to buy and ship computers and other technical equipment to their offices in Indonesia and India.

Prior to the actual printing and production of the cards and calendars, we would coordinate with UNICEF New York on the pre-production materials such as design and artwork. This was of course slightly more complicated in the days before digital files!

We were also communicating with the Regional Office in Bangkok and other UNICEF offices in the region about their orders of cards and gifts. The orders then had to be shipped to several ports in the region such as Manila, Jakarta, Yangon, Karachi, New Delhi and Tokyo.

Later, the Singapore office was mandated to print and distribute UNICEF greeting cards and other products for the National Committees for UNICEF in Australia and New Zealand as well.

Previously, the then Singapore Council of Social Service (SCSS)[1] had been responsible for the local sales of UNICEF greeting cards. After it decided to produce and sell its own greeting cards, UNICEF greeting cards were no longer the main focus and sales began to decline. With the establishment of the UNICEF Singapore office in 1986, the local marketing and sales functions were taken over by this new office. There was a sales outlet in our small office on Orchard Road and additional sales points and stands in shopping centres during the lead-up to seasonal celebrations. Soon after I arrived in Singapore, UNICEF launched the production and sale of Chinese New Year cards, in addition to the Christmas cards that UNICEF was already known for worldwide. This followed UNICEF's practice of responding to the demands of local markets.

Private sector fundraising through direct mailings was not well appreciated by the charity sector in Singapore at that time, but it was probably something that would have appealed to a number of ordinary people like those who, after having seen or heard some media coverage on TV or the radio, would come to our office spontaneously and donate money for a special UNICEF programme in a given country or natural disaster like an earthquake or flooding. There were

---

[1] The SCSS was restructured and renamed the National Council of Social Service (NCSS) in 1992.

also university students who devised a fundraising effort for UNICEF programmes by creating a giant jigsaw puzzle in public, selling the puzzle parts to local companies and handing over a big cheque to me at the end. It was a marvellous action showing to me the great empathy that these young Singaporeans had for others beyond their borders.

The nature of the UNICEF presence in a country is dependent on the situation of its children. In developing countries, UNICEF offices implement programmes of cooperation that are agreed with national governments and based on jointly identified priority programme areas under the leadership of a Representative. In developed economies, often the National Committees for UNICEF[2] and civil society organisations will raise public awareness and conduct fundraising for UNICEF programmes in developing countries around the world. At that time, Singapore was in transition. The government no longer needed UNICEF's assistance for its social programmes for children, so there were no longer UNICEF programme activities. At the same time, there was no National Committee for UNICEF yet. Therefore, I also performed some representation work, with support from the Regional Office in Bangkok, to present aspects of UNICEF's work in government meetings, schools, companies, organisations and the media.

From my personal experience, people living on islands often have the tendency not to look as much over "the edge of their plate" as much as people who live with solid borders with their neighbours. However, Singapore, a relatively small place with a big harbour, managed this "handicap" rather well and became a global player, inviting investments and companies from all over the world.

This kind of spirit — of "looking over the edge of one's own plate" that I witnessed in Singapore — is sorely needed as our world is growing closer over issues (such as climate change, globalisation, environmental preservation, renewable energy sources and water security) that can often not be dealt with locally and need global cooperation and common approaches. I would very much like to especially encourage young Singaporeans to contribute their enthusiasm and to share ideas and plans with persons and organisations around the world.

Looking back, from my point of view, at that time there were some practices and procedures in Singapore that were puzzling and seemed somewhat excessive; such as the length of time it took for my work permit to be approved and the censorship of parts of German news magazines I used to subscribe to. I was also

---

[2] The National Committees are an integral part of UNICEF's global organisation and a unique feature of UNICEF. Currently there are 36 National Committees in the world, each established as an independent local non-governmental organisation.

fascinated by the efforts of the government to provide opportunities for young graduates to socialise, to try and encourage them to get married and have children. This was done in an effort to help counter the falling birth rates in the country.

It could be that at the time Singapore was a young nation, about 25 years of age then, still insecure and more than usually sensitive. It is difficult to know what impact more political opposition and loosening controls would have had on the impressive achievements over the last 50 years.

All these unconventional features could however not diminish my admiration for what Mr Lee Kuan Yew and his government had already achieved in nation-building in such a short time. To mention but a few — an efficient administration, a very good infrastructure (streets, underground and other public transport, airline, port), a high level of education, excellent programmes to create home ownership through pension fund savings (a programme which, in my view, should be exported to many places in the world), and stable, reliable conditions for local and international businesses.

Apart from the efficient conditions for business some of the things we most enjoyed about Singapore were the wonderful relaxing zoo (where we soon became members as "Friends of the Zoo" and took our guests), the East Coast with its beaches and restaurants, Chinatown, Little India and the island of Sentosa. Singapore was also an ideal place from which to visit neighbouring places such as the Malaysian islands of Rawa, Pulau Besar, Tioman and Langkawi, Sumatra in Indonesia, and cities like Bangkok and Perth.

Finally, I would like to congratulate Singapore and its entire people on its 50th anniversary and wish them all the best and a continuation to become, with its excellent manpower and resources, an even stronger partner in world affairs in the future.

I survived the humid heat in Singapore. After just four weeks on this wonderful island in the sun I was already playing tennis at the Dutch Club during lunch breaks! Apparently, my brain and body had adjusted successfully.

From Geneva to Singapore:
Sales Support to National Partners

Penny Whitworth

Penny Whitworth worked in the UNICEF Singapore office as Greeting Card Operation Manager from 1991 to 1994 and Market Development Officer Asia from 1994 to 1998. In this essay she speaks of the evolution of the sales of UNICEF greeting cards and the role the UNICEF Singapore office played in sales.

In 1975 I joined what was then the UNICEF Greeting Card Operation in Geneva, Switzerland.

In those days the division, with its headquarters in New York, was responsible for sourcing, producing and distributing the cards, calendars and gifts to National Committees for UNICEF and a number of UNICEF Country Offices that were responsible for sales in their respective countries. It was early days for providing marketing and sales support beyond bespoke publicity and promotion materials. The prime areas of expertise at headquarters at that time were the fine arts, printing, production, logistics and promotion. The majority of sales were carried out through volunteers at points of sale such as shopping centres, markets and bazaars. There was little commercial distribution, and sales to companies for their corporate greetings were just beginning. Volunteers were particularly important outside of the capital cities.

In the late 1970s the impact of UNICEF greeting cards and gifts were synonymous with the reputation and distinction of the organisation. They presented escalating and abundant opportunities to engage with a variety of audiences and to augment awareness and support for UNICEF's work to help children survive, protect them from harm and get them to school. Senior UNICEF management decided to apply its hallmark strategy; research good practices, adapt and apply them to engaging the worldwide greeting card market to the fullest extent possible. Experienced marketing and managerial professionals from blue chip companies were recruited, market research agencies were engaged and existing staff members like myself went to Business Management schools to acquire the training and skills required for this more industry-type engagement. At first we analysed the existing sales channels and methods and established benchmarks from which to work and compare performance inter and intra markets.

In the 1980s the international support team was assembled. We developed and implemented with our national partners an annual marketing plan for each country by which sales were increased and performance improved. We carried out regular market research, including annual product and pricing checks on each market to make sure that UNICEF cards were competitive in addition to being leading edge. In the 1990s, consumer research expanded to include focus groups to probe existing and potential UNICEF cards and gifts buyers about their purchasing preferences including where they liked to shop, the different types of motifs, treatments and sizes and about their knowledge and understanding of UNICEF and its work. This market research was carried out regularly, often at costs that were heavily discounted by our partners. It influenced our strategies to develop appropriate ranges in different countries, distribute them in easy to locate outlets and increase market shares. By the time I left Geneva in 1991 for Singapore I was responsible for representing 12 markets in West Europe and 20 markets in East Africa, in 1990 the sales revenue for those markets reached US$40 million.

Regional Production and Logistics, Singapore

The United Nations has a policy of promoting job mobility. After 15 years in various market development functions in Geneva, I was asked to relocate to the Singapore office to supervise the production and distribution of UNICEF cards, gifts and catalogues for approximately 20 countries in the Asia and Pacific regions. In addition I was to lead the team to increase income from the private sector in Singapore through UNICEF product sales and fundraising and to promote the work and aims of UNICEF through information and advocacy campaigns principally with the mass media and educational establishments.

The majority of my assignments in Singapore at that time related to production and distribution. It was necessary for me to think and act differently. I had worked with a number of multidisciplinary teams in Geneva to assess opportunities to enhance our operations and increase the amount of funds for programmes for children including integrated production, distribution and point of sale systems based on barcoding, a feature today that has been perfected by the likes of Amazon. This was good preparation for my initial assignment to Singapore. Perhaps the best grounding was to apply the established UNICEF approach which is to assess the best practices in the domain, adapt them where appropriate for the context, test and then implement them.

The small team in the office was experienced, skilled, knowledgeable and incredibly kind and generous in their welcome. From the outset we established excellent working and personal relations with regular social interactions including sampling the food courts and sometimes the restaurants close by the office at least once a week for lunch.

While the operational functions of the office were well covered by a veteran print manager with a keen eye for colour register, and two expert assistants for administration and distribution, there was just one person to run the seasonal sales campaign.

The production team worked closely with the headquarters to ensure that printing and packaging standards were consistent. All the operations were out-sourced to leading suppliers. In the days before digital printing techniques, pre-print materials arrived from New York by courier and approvals were given for print, often during the night. For the elaborate embossed and debossed cards, frequently in gold, sometimes silver, printers specialised in high-end printing for the perfume industry were engaged. Otherwise the leading printers met the quality and performance criteria required for UNICEF cards and promotion materials. The machinery and scheduling methods were the same as those I had encountered in Europe. The fresh approaches I brought to the process were to advance the interests and concerns of our sales partners and their customers, using marketing and logistics experience to provide useful perspectives in resolving issues and identifying cross-sectoral efficiencies and cost-savings.

This was an overriding principle for me in the field of packing and shipping the items to sales partners. It was complex and the suppliers in Singapore were thoroughly practised to service a variety of climates, administrations and cultures in addition to the special privileges and immunities associated to property of a United Nations agency. Over a period of months spent reviewing the logistical arrangements and suppliers we used, meeting with and learning from potential vendors for out-sourcing and constantly reminding ourselves of what it meant to be an end consumer of these services, the team managed to re-engineer the business, improve efficiency and save costs. We were in the vicinity of the port area on a regular basis, and the constant manipulation of the 20 and 40 ft containers was always an awe-inspiring spectacle as was the never-ending line of ships along the east coast that looked like a city from the distance. I would love to have been taken on a tour of the working port and harbour of Singapore.

Public Outreach, Singapore

To achieve sales increases it was essential to augment and train a group of active volunteers. Equally important to our effort was to make sure that the volunteers understood and knew UNICEF work sufficiently well to articulate key messages and ideas to anyone they met in the course of their tasks. Increasing sales went hand in hand with increasing awareness and understanding for the problems facing children around the world and the work of UNICEF to help children survive and thrive, from early childhood through adolescence.

This would have been a near impossible task and certainly would have been on a far smaller scale if the sales coordinator had been someone other than Peggy Kek. She brought skills, experience and enthusiasm to the job that were engaging and inspirational. This meant countless evening and weekend sessions, written and live appeals through the media, seizing every opportunity that presented itself to meet and speak with anybody and everybody who was willing to listen and who had access to a readily available network. Our operations colleagues doubled up their efforts to support this new thrust of engagement, energetically embracing new public-oriented assignments and servicing the requirements of a new audience.

The outreach was diverse, the response enthusiastic and the resulting collaboration abundant. Sales increased and a variety of community based and led volunteer initiatives became regular features in the life of UNICEF Singapore. The reactions were as we expected and no less wholehearted than elsewhere in the world. Most people were troubled by the stories of vulnerable children and were eager to join together to help bring change. Over time we were hopeful that this could lead to a more enduring support presence in Singapore, possibly along the lines of a National Committee for UNICEF. In the meantime, increased revenues enabled us to convert the temporary position into a fixed position for general development. A number of the events and collaborations are described elsewhere in this book. In 1993 sales revenue increased by 23% and donations by 75%.

Regional Resource Mobilisation, Singapore

In the meantime, with changing technology and the global economy, the regional production centres in Singapore and Rio de Janeiro became less viable and cost-effective. As the UNICEF regional production centre was phased out in Singapore, UNICEF Singapore became a hub for the development and strengthening for sales and fundraising from the private sector in Asia for Country Offices. The same happened in Rio de Janeiro to the regional hub for Latin America and the Caribbean Country Offices. At a later date both hubs were consolidated into the respective regional offices of UNICEF in Bangkok and Panama City.

The renewed office was responsible to advise selected Country Offices on marketing strategies and the sales of UNICEF cards and gifts, and fundraising activities including planning and operational management. The principal objectives were to maximise private sector net income in close collaboration with each Country Office and Global Headquarters with the responsibility to define the right product line and promotional support to ensure profitable and strategic use of limited investments. This was also true for private sector fundraising recommendations and performance in the assigned countries as well as to ensure consistency with global strategic direction as approved by the Executive Board of UNICEF. The office was augmented with a General Manager and experts in fundraising development, IT and production control for the region. I took on the regional market development role working with markets from Pakistan to the Philippines.

Some Country Offices had been active in the sale of UNICEF cards and gifts for many years with professional sales and marketing individuals recruited to manage and develop sales in larger markets and in some cases logistics professionals were hired to ensure efficient distribution throughout the country. Sales had grown over the years following similar distribution patterns and principles as for National Committees, as was the practice in Singapore. The same principle of being close to market drove the establishment of the Regional Support Centres as they were known. As country offices became more active in sales and then fundraising from individuals, companies and organisations, their role expanded to advocacy and communications with new target audiences. One of the challenges for some in the country offices was to assimilate consumer research and brand communications to existing systems and procedures for programme communications and advocacy.

The practical and institutional aspects of my new job were very similar to those in Geneva. I worked with national counterparts, who for the most part were seasoned sales professionals from the private sector, on the development, design, planning and operational management for UNICEF of marketing strategies and sales activities in India, Pakistan Indonesia, Thailand, Malaysia, the Philippines, China and Singapore. This included supervising the regional and national work plans and budgets as well as market research and assessment. The significant change for me was in the distribution and market conditions. There was a much heavier reliance on commercial sales channels and, what were for UNICEF, significant margins to the retailers and distributors.

The India market in particular was highly competitive with a thriving card printing sector that was closely associated with the British commercial and charity card networks, some of the most powerful in the world. It was not unusual to be walking down the street to come across sales kiosks carrying designs that were available in the UK being sold out of cardboard cartons alongside other cards. To increase the net earnings for programmes we started to focus on direct sales to companies, the prime targets being the multinational companies that were existing customers in other parts of the world. We also researched the much sought-after "middle class" of India at the time. Direct mail catalogue sales were in their infancy in India at that time. Accessing reliable databases, personalising the mailings and processing the orders all presented challenges to our customer service standards. Issues that today are solved seamlessly took months of cross-sectoral research and testing, and included negotiating with banks and credit card companies. Another example would be how to merge mailing lists of thousands of names and fuse them with emerging digital printing techniques for personalisation and then link those to in-house inventory and order fulfilment processes that remained manual.

It is my experience that the UNICEF sales teams, salaried and volunteer, in every country are talented, resourceful professionals endowed with endless energy and enthusiasm. They are generous with their knowledge, time and friendship and always ready to walk the extra mile to make a sale and raise additional funds for programmes. They are a treasure that I value and am fortunate to have worked with.

In 1996, net proceeds from sales increased by 11%.

Moving on From Singapore

On a personal level, moving to Singapore catapulted me to a new and different way of acting and thinking. I arrived, not knowing anyone, in a new culture, to carry out an expanded role in a small office and to find a new home. I suspect Singapore strikes most newcomers as a modern cityscape with the same amenities, facilities and entertainment as any other cosmopolitan city, with the added advantages of convenience and efficiency. I never got used to the rapid urban transformations with streets changing overnight and the equally rapid number of new acronyms. I quickly learned that a number of rituals, attitudes and behaviour from past eras co-existed relatively comfortably with the quest for all the progress, convenience and sophistication of consumerism that the 21st century has to offer. This was exciting with sometimes puzzling dynamics. I started reading local and regional authors and attending theatrical performances. The content and tone were entirely fresh and sometimes startling. Social commentary and observation were woven into the creative process, performances and narrative. I was fortunate enough to know some of the leading players in the field of theatre and many other exceptional people in Singapore.

William Teo springs to mind as a wonderful example of these encounters. What a generous, gifted, thoughtful and thought-provoking human being. William founded Asia-in-Theatre Research Circus and was one of the pioneers of Singapore's English-language theatre in the 1980s and 1990s. My story with William is fairly representative of my many serendipitous moments in Singapore. I came to William through the Alliance Francaise, a rich supply of Francophone resources for me in the early days. It also became a great supporter of UNICEF hosting exhibitions and sales events. At first William worked wonders with my hair in his salon. Then he introduced me to his other passion and vocation — his marvellous theatre creations. Some were performed in a disused warehouse, magically converted to convey other worlds. Like the rest of the audience I was led through a flow of cultures from France, through Cambodia and India in thoroughly distinctive and finely-crafted writing, staging and performance. It was enchanting. I shall never forget the production of *Macbeth*. William too became a staunch supporter of UNICEF, cards were promoted and sold at his hair salon and theatre performances. On one occasion he invited us to organise a small exhibition at a performance, the proceeds of which he donated to UNICEF. In those days it was difficult to sustain a full-time career in the arts even for leading artists.

When you move from one place to another the hardest thing to do is to leave your friends and colleagues behind. This was true when I left Singapore for New York. I had spent seven rich years of discovery and gained tremendously in learning and experience. I still yearn for the freshly squeezed fruit juices and wonder whether the noisy calls of tree frogs on the East Coast still startle the evening visitors.

A Swede in Singapore

Per-Olov Lennartsson with Penny Whitworth[1]

Per-Olov Lennartsson was the UNICEF Regional Greeting Card Operation Manager for Asia in Singapore from August 1994 to December 1996. He was responsible for a team of 10 persons that provided technical advice, specialised training and administrative support to 19 UNICEF Country Offices in Asia on how to raise funds from the private sector. Here, he shares his experience and a number of insights into the differences between his assignments in UNICEF Country and Regional Offices in East Africa and in the UNICEF Office in Singapore.

I first joined UNICEF in July 1975 as Assistant Programme Officer in Colombo, Sri Lanka where I was responsible for administration, finance, personnel and the supply and purchasing functions to cover UNICEF's humanitarian assistance in Sri Lanka and the Maldives. I stayed in that position for approximately three years. Three to four years in a country was to be the pattern for my career with UNICEF before arriving in Singapore.

I then worked in Ethiopia, Uganda and Kenya. In Kenya, I was working in the UNICEF regional office that supported 21 countries in the region. We helped the offices to mobilise adequate financial and human resources so that UNICEF could offer optimal programmes for children and women. The programme areas that I supervised depended on the situation of the children in each country and the priorities agreed with the government. They included Health, Water and Sanitation, Nutrition, Social Statistics and Emergencies.

I went to Singapore in 1994 to take up the post of the Greeting Card Operation Manager for the Asia region. The principal brief of the UNICEF team in Singapore

[1] This account is based on a series of email interviews by Penny Whitworth from April to July 2015.

was to provide professional advice and assistance to our Country Offices in Asia to raise funds in the private sector. We were supporting 19 offices in the region.

In light of the rapid economic development and the rise of a thriving civic society in many Asian countries during the 1980s and the 1990s, UNICEF believed that the potential to generate considerable amounts of revenues within many countries had increased. Such additional financial resources could significantly strengthen the country's capacity to meet the basic needs of its inhabitants in general and children and mothers in particular.

Furthermore, UNICEF continued to advocate for a more progressive tax system to mobilise more financial resources for expanding the social sector.

The main functions of the Singapore Office were to advise, guide and assist the Asian Country Offices to: increase their financial resources by continuing and intensifying the current successful strategy of marketing a wide range of products; and to develop and introduce new ways of direct fund raising.

In addition, our office was responsible for the quality control of products manufactured in Asia, mainly in China, for sale around the world. At that point, the UNICEF merchandise that was being produced in Asia included greeting cards, diaries and mugs.

The main factors for choosing Singapore as a base for UNICEF's efforts to establish a regional support centre for expanding fundraising activities within Asian countries were: The existence of a well-functioning office, which had established and maintained close and efficient collaboration with printing companies delivering greeting cards for worldwide distribution; a well-organised and efficiently maintained infrastructure serving regional and global needs; and in particular the existence of an international airport which offered frequent, direct flights to almost all capitals in Asia.

The challenges were quite different to what I had experienced before.

Fundraising was a new field for some Heads of UNICEF Offices in the Asian countries. This meant that in addition to providing operational and technical support for income-generating programmes, we also provided basic introductions to resource mobilisation from the private sector and guidance on how to integrate fundraising into core programmes such as advocacy areas.

However, country offices were stretched to the limit by multiple demands and emerging complexities of child protection including trafficking, sexual exploitation, labour, and the ratification and implementation of the Convention on the Rights of the Child to survival and development.

This left limited time to introduce new programmes and processes, even though they were based on successful models of fundraising for UNICEF from other countries, including South America.

The Singapore office served in an advisory capacity. It didn't have a mandate to implement. This meant that in some instances, the planning and implementation phases took longer than anticipated and resulted in lower levels of income than initially expected.

During this period, after careful market research and assessment of market potential in seven countries (China, India, Indonesia, Malaysia, Pakistan, the Philippines and Thailand) we developed and implemented a regional private sector fundraising strategy. The region now contributes more than US$50 million a year to children. Net profits from the existing sales campaigns of cards and gift items in the region increased by over 10%.

On the personal front, Singapore also presented a number of changes to my family and me. Most of my previous duty stations were in the capitals of so-called least developed countries. From our arrival as a family in Singapore we were struck by how everything was extremely well organised. We will never forget that as soon as we signed the lease for our apartment and made the deposit, the electricity and gas system immediately flowed in our apartment. We had never before experienced such a well-coordinated and efficient organisation even when living in highly developed countries.

From earlier duty stations we were used to living with unreliable telephone lines, daily power and water cuts, disruptions to transport and food shortages. Such factors could negatively affect work and private life.

Power cuts meant that we kept at least two buckets of water in the bathroom (for the toilet, shower and hand basin) for when the water pump could not function. We learned to open and close the fridge door very quickly to grab perishables and in the office, to save documents on the computer every two minutes to avoid losing them. Generally there was a shortage of food items, at least the kind of food we as foreigners were used to: milk, sugar and wheat flour were hard to find and when we managed to find a piece of cheese it was like "New Year's Eve".

In Africa, as foreigners we were fortunate to possess a car of our own and did not have to rely on the public transport system that was more prone to fail due to the difficulties we all had in finding petrol. This forced us to use the car for only the absolutely necessary, essential trips. Practically every month there was a shortage of petrol and once the news was spread about the availability of petrol at one or two stations, everyone stopped working and quickly got into the car and drove off to the station to queue up to fill the tank.

In Singapore, the contrast was immense, we all moved easily by public transport at a nominal cost and with limited air pollution to work, school and for leisure activities.

In all countries we were very privileged compared with the majority of the inhabitants. With a water tank on top of the roof, which was fairly quickly filled up, once the electricity had returned and provided that the pump was in good order, we had running water. In Singapore we could have a shower any time of the day.

In Africa we had little need for an alarm clock in the morning. Our neighbour's cockerel was always alert and persistent until everyone was out of the bed. In some places the cockerel could face hard competition from the announcer in the minaret. In Singapore however an alarm clock was a must, at least in our family.

Despite the daily challenges we experienced in African countries, compared to the stable, comfortable living and working conditions in Singapore or our own country Sweden, we were never frustrated or found any reasons for serious complaints. Not everyone shared our enthusiasm and point of view.

I remember Singapore was much commercialised with impressive, rapid economic development which the country had undergone since its independence half a century ago. We were amazed to find anything mostly without any time delay and easily; household and IT equipment, and clothes of any kind. Food items from any corner of the globe, e.g., cheese from Switzerland, milk from Australia. We often wondered how such abundance of all these items might have influenced the life style and values of many of its citizens. It seemed to us that, in common with countries of a similar standard of living, awareness of overconsumption and reliance on unsustainable resources was low. It was a very bright contrast to the levels of consumption and living conditions in the economically underdeveloped countries we had experienced for almost two decades.

As my wife and I were born and raised in the countryside we like to spend as much time as possible in quiet places far away from overcrowded and busy places. We enjoyed immensely visiting remote and quiet islands in the Singaporean archipelago. In all capitals in Africa we were fortunate to have easy access to nature. Even in the capital cities we could see magnificent birds whose cousins seem to have almost been brought to extinction in places like Singapore and other heavily urbanised cities and countries, or through modern farming practices and misguided hunting.

On a less happy note, in Singapore each year we experienced periods of high levels of air pollution (so-called "haze") caused by the large-scale burning of land in neighbouring islands of Indonesia. This resulted in serious health problems for people in Singapore and other nearby countries. Unfortunately the situation appears to have remained and still causes considerable health, social and economic problems.

But back to UNICEF. Singapore being a high-tech, wealthy city-state offered several favourable conditions for UNICEF's work. As a regional and global hub, its well-developed infrastructure, abundance of well-educated and experienced national staff were positive factors in ensuring smooth operations. The housing facilities and education system were very beneficial factors for international staff members.

In Africa, at work, without phones, our contact with government officials and representatives of partner organisations had to be done by personal visits.

The permanent shortage of fuel meant that UNICEF staff at times could not travel out of the capital to implement and monitor programmes for children and women. When these trips could take place, vehicles were loaded with six to eight so-called "jerry cans" of fuel to make sure that the team not only reached the intended destinations but avoided being stranded outside the capital.

In some countries implementation of UNICEF's operations was seriously delayed as money could not be transferred from the capital to sub-offices due to a non-existent or poorly functioning banking system. As a consequence, funds to pay salaries and programme costs were transported by car from the capital to the provinces. To distant sub-offices UNICEF used to hire small aeroplanes to transport the money.

A major factor in making my tour of duty in Singapore rewarding and memorable was the high level of professionalism and maturity of the staff members of UNICEF. Their wealth of initiative, openness and commitment to UNICEF's mandate and goal were crucial factors in creating a stimulating working environment and positive atmosphere.

Our relations with the Ministry of Foreign Affairs were cordial and mutually respectful. We were however unsuccessful in engaging the Singaporean government in a dialogue which could have allowed UNICEF to more actively access the great potential for raising funds and general support within the country to be used as humanitarian assistance in other less economically developed countries. As a result, the anticipated increase in close and constructive collaboration with the government, civil society and voluntary organisations of Singapore did not materialise. Hence UNICEF Singapore's work from the mid-1990s focused on providing support and guidance to other countries in Asia.

Considering however the recognised talent, knowledge and skills of many Singaporeans and the magnitude of the country's accumulated financial resources, it was a pity that we could not have done more within Singapore. The government contribution towards UNICEF's Regular Resources (RR) has been around US$50,000 for many years.[2]

The enthusiastic and generous contributions from institutions and individuals were constant. One example that affirms this good support and intentions of civil society in Singapore towards the UN and UNICEF during my term was a dinner held in 1995 to commemorate the 50th anniversary of the ratification of the UN Charter. It was held on United Nations Day, 24th October and organised by the United Nations Association of Singapore, to benefit UNICEF, UNDP and UNHCR.

In Singapore we admired the deliberate efforts from the outset of the nation to successfully integrate all members of the community, something that many countries facing mass immigration could learn. This is demonstrated clearly in one of our fondest memories of Singapore, the many evenings we enjoyed dinner at different food centres (locally called "hawker centres"). With its rich multicultural heritage, Singapore serves up a true melting pot of flavours and foods. While enjoying delicious dishes like lamb vindaloo, chicken biryani or nasi goreng we were privileged to join with many Singaporeans at table and gain unique insights to their daily lives. As we have always been keen to try to adjust to new situations and being interested in all kinds of food, for us, this was an important ingredient in getting to know alternative ways of living and associated cultures.

---

[2] See Annex 2 of "A Brief History" on p. xxxvii.

My Journey to Singapore with UNICEF

Jackie Leung

Jackie Leung left Oxfam and Hong Kong in 1997 to take up a new job at UNICEF in Singapore. In this essay she reflects on her beliefs in empowering communities to help themselves, and her role as a UNICEF regional fundraising coordinator for Southeast Asia.

I'm writing this essay on a day very special to me. Today I attended a Citizenship Ceremony and formally became a Singaporean, although the citizenship was already granted about one year ago and I have been a Permanent Resident for many years.

And marking this milestone of my life on the 50th anniversary of this young country makes it all that more significant. 2015 is a special number to every Singaporean. And to me. It has been a meaningful journey ever since I first set sail. And I never looked back. It all began some 18 years ago. UNICEF was the first chapter.

I was the Fundraising Coordinator for Oxfam Hong Kong back then. My team and I ran all the fundraising programmes and events in Hong Kong to support its many poverty alleviation programmes in developing countries, mostly in Asia. In Oxfam, an international development non-governmental agency, the mission is to help people help themselves. I strongly believe that in every community and every social problem, the solutions largely lie in the power of the people themselves. Show them the way and give them the tools. People can be empowered to help each other.

While carrying out my fundraising and publicity work, I witnessed the accomplishment of many rural programmes in various Asian poor communities that strengthened further my deep conviction. So when I was invited to consider the post of regional fundraising officer at the UNICEF office in Singapore in 1996, I responded without hesitation. The idea of rallying support from developing countries to help their own fellow people excited me. And being able to promote this in Asia makes it so much more meaningful as it is home to me. At the same time, I was attracted by the opportunity as much as the country where the office was in: Singapore.

Soon after the interview I was offered the job. In March 1997, I relocated to Singapore. It was four months before the historical event of the Hong Kong handover back to China by the British. Speculation and unsettled sentiments filled the air of the little "Pearl of the Orient" during that period. Many people had packed their way out. Many more were thinking about it. I left my hometown at a very emotional time. I could imagine how others would have speculated about my motive. But I knew from the bottom of my heart, my decision had nothing to do with the changeover. The timing was pure coincidence. As it turned out, I am just happy that I took the chance. It led to a new life. Looking back, 1997 was another special number to me. It was a watershed moment for my hometown. And for my personal life.

I remember my first surprise was to find out that the small UNICEF regional office was located right on bustling Orchard Road, albeit at the quieter end of the street. It was next to the Thai Embassy, in International Building, on the ninth floor. Coming from a non-governmental organisation (NGO) background, I was used to more "humble" office locations such as old housing areas, far away from subway stations and so on. But Orchard Road was and still is a busy and up-market shopping zone in Singapore. We were surrounded by malls and hotels.

Of course later I found out there was a good reason for that. In Singapore, UNICEF's core business of public fundraising was selling greeting cards. So the office also served as a shop. Being in a convenient spot made it easier for customers to walk in to make their purchases and for volunteers to gather and help out. Remember back then online shopping was still very new. Amazon.com had gone online only in mid-1995. About a year later we moved to a slightly bigger office in another building called Forum on the other side of the road. One reason for the move was that Forum was known as a child-friendly shopping centre. That image fitted well with the child-focused mission of UNICEF. I thought that was a good marketing edge.

My work was mainly to assist the programme country offices in the region to start up and develop their local fundraising programmes. Traditionally the

UNICEF offices of these developing countries had been on the receiving end of funds that came mostly from foreign sources. At the time that I joined UNICEF, there was a new initiative in the organisation to try and explore other means of funding support, especially from the growing private sector in these countries, for their local programmes. It was a very exciting new direction and I was delighted to be part of the start-up process.

I would make regular visits to the UNICEF offices of a few Southeast Asian countries, including Thailand, the Philippines and Indonesia. I also accompanied a delegation to visit the Hong Kong Committee to observe its fundraising programmes and to UNICEF Manila to observe fundraising programmes and a UNICEF-assisted project.

Although our regional office did not actively initiate any fundraising in Singapore, from time to time there would be requests from schools and organisations to raise funds for UNICEF projects. I would say, on the whole, people in Singapore were much more aware of UNICEF greeting cards and thus would normally offer their support by buying cards.

In the course of those two years, we worked on a few new schemes such as monthly donation programmes by direct mail and corporate events. I also helped on staff training, country annual planning and conducted feasibility research.

During the time that I spent in the regional UNICEF office, I learnt as many things as I had to offer in the relatively new position. Apart from the cultural adaptation and personal life adjustment, the biggest change on the job was that I changed from being very in touch with the field and frontline happenings to doing almost all the work over email and papers. The actions and scenes became words and numbers. At times I felt that my grasp of each market situation was somewhat indirect and not as timely as I wanted it to be as I relied on the information fed by the country fundraising manager. Luckily we had very capable and motivated staff from country offices such as Thailand and the Philippines. They both had relevant private sector experience prior to joining UNICEF.

Being in a regional supporting role also gave me a chance to learn how to see things in a more macro perspective, to understand how different cultures may affect charitable behaviour, etc. It was also my role to build a network of rapport and facilitate the sharing of experiences among the countries, and to explore training opportunities for staff members both within UNICEF and through programmes outside.

There was no lack of challenges to overcome while pushing forward the concept of public fundraising in and outside of local UNICEF offices at my time. It was partly due to the novelty of the idea, and partly because of the lack of infrastructure such as a reliable mailing and financial services system to run a monthly donation programme. There was also an absence of a sizeable middle-class population, a lack of a good understanding among the general public of what programmes UNICEF was carrying out in their country and so on. With the limited manpower resources (one manager and one assistant in each country) to cover the entire nation, we had to work wisely to achieve cost effectiveness and optimal results. Corporate fundraising would be a primary area that got more attention. Not only because large corporations have the financial muscle, but also because we could, through their big workforce, promote the work and values that UNICEF represents to the local people. Fundraising and advocacy work hand in hand. And that was exactly what we were attempting to do in those years. By understanding the issues in their own country, people could respond (by making a small donation or helping in a fundraising event) and being part of the solution to their own problem.

To be able to achieve this mission, it was paramount to have the country management to share this vision and lend their unreserved support to the local fundraising team. The funds raised were mostly channelled to local programmes and projects related to basic health programmes such as polio eradication, sodium deficiency-related diseases, vaccination programmes for mothers and children and so on.

Back in the little Lion City, our regional team was also going through a long adjustment time in the 1990s. The head of office who was also my first boss, Edward Spescha, had finished his term and left Singapore shortly after I arrived. He was a wise and senior person in UNICEF and like a mentor to me during the few months we worked together. After that, for a long time, the hat was taken up by our very dynamic senior greeting card officer, Penny Whitworth, who had to oversee the whole UNICEF office operation in addition to her primary area of responsibility of promoting greeting card sales in the region. Penny had to travel extensively to five or six countries. Many times I remembered she would take an overnight flight back from Pakistan, go home to shower, and then go straight to the office for another day of work. Her unfailing smile and constant energy was what kept everyone steady and close together.

Not having to travel as much as my greeting card colleague, I actually found the time to revive some old hobbies that I had left off years ago such as calligraphy, hiking and Cantonese opera singing. Later, through my opera singing, I met a fellow amateur opera artiste and drama actor who would go on to become my husband. Being Chinese, raised in my own culture, involved in the traditional arts for many years and now married to a large local family in Singapore, has provided a first-hand perspective for me to see how the culture of Singapore is quickly evolving.

Singapore is an incredibly fast-growing country. It has achieved in just 50 years what many countries took centuries to do. Many things that were perceived as foreign and new have today become part of life. For example, many of the "pioneer generation" (a term that the Singapore government uses to describe the first generation that helped to build the country from the 1960s) don't speak English. Their mother tongue is either a Chinese dialect, Malay or Tamil. Today all Singaporeans speak English.

But not all younger Singapore Chinese can speak fluent dialect or read and write in Mandarin, sometimes affecting their ability to link to their cultural roots and to appreciate tradition. With the rise of China however, there is renewed appreciation of the Chinese language and culture.

Singapore has risen as a vibrant and successful economy in the last few decades. The skyline has almost completely changed from 18 years ago when I first set foot on this place. People's understanding of their country identity and their relations to neighbouring countries has progressed a lot especially for the younger generations. From my personal encounters with the young people here, many of them have joined missions to travel to other poorer communities as volunteers to help build houses, teach English, or for emergency relief work, etc. I think there's a readiness to reach out and help, and to learn about what's happening in other neighbouring communities. More so than before surely. It would be meaningful if UNICEF would strengthen its presence here in Singapore to let people know more about its many important programmes and offer a way for people to respond.

The UNICEF regional office is in Bangkok now, no longer in Singapore. But just like the way UNICEF touches many lives around the world, working with and for children, it has brought important changes in mine. And it never feels far away from me. On my desk there's always my navy blue UNICEF coffee mug. Last week I wrote a UNICEF card for my niece in London; I never miss a chance to buy some when I stumble upon new stock. You shouldn't either.

UNICEF Goodwill Ambassador Danny Kaye entertains children outside the Rehabilitation Hospital in Tokyo, Japan. Kaye also visited Singapore in 1971. Credit: © UNICEF/NYHQ1961-0004/Unknown

An inscription of James P. Grant, UNICEF's third Executive Director, at UNICEF House in New York.
Credit: Dinia del Sol

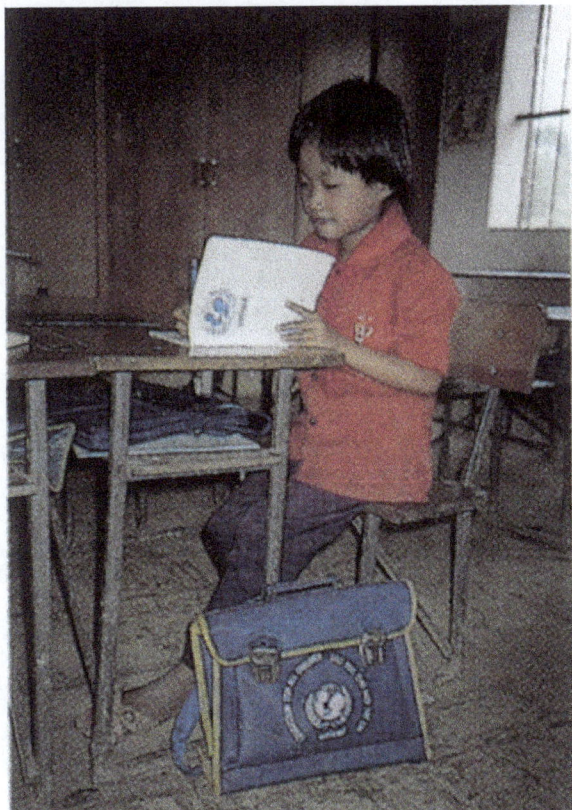

Vietnamese girl with her UNICEF-supported school bag and stationery (1994). Credit: Peggy Kek

Cheng Wing-Sie with Meena, the Girls' Education Mascot and her brother Raju, at a UNICEF-supported event to raise awareness of gender equality in Nepal (2000).

First Day Cover stamps issued by Singapore to mark Children's Day in 1974. The stamps feature drawings by Singaporean kindergarten children.
Credit: Singapore Philatelic Museum

The painting, *Mother and Daughter*, by Cheong Soo Pieng was featured in a UNICEF First Day Cover in 1981.
Credit: UNICEF, Quek Tse-Kwang

The painting, *Mother and Daughter*, by Cheong Soo Pieng was featured in a UNICEF First Day Cover in 1981.
Credit: Quek Tse-Kwang

SSPA Project Gansu Province (1996) UNICEF staff Dr Ng Shui-Meng (seated, taking notes) conducting household interviews to assess women's needs prior to loan approval.

SSPA Project Shaanxi Province (2000) UNICEF staff Dr Ng Shui-Meng (seated left in black jacket) visiting a women's group to assess loan-use results.

School children lining up outside a classroom in a UNICEF-assisted school in northern Vietnam (1994). Credit: Peggy Kek

Dr Ng Shui-Meng (far right) with children from poor families in the fields near their homes (Social Development Project, Shigatse County, China's Tibet Autonomous Region, circa 1999).

Regional Conference on Children of Urban Families in Singapore in 1994. Front row, 8th and 9th from left: Dr Khoo Kim Choo and Sheldon Shaeffer from UNICEF.
Credit: Khoo Kim Choo

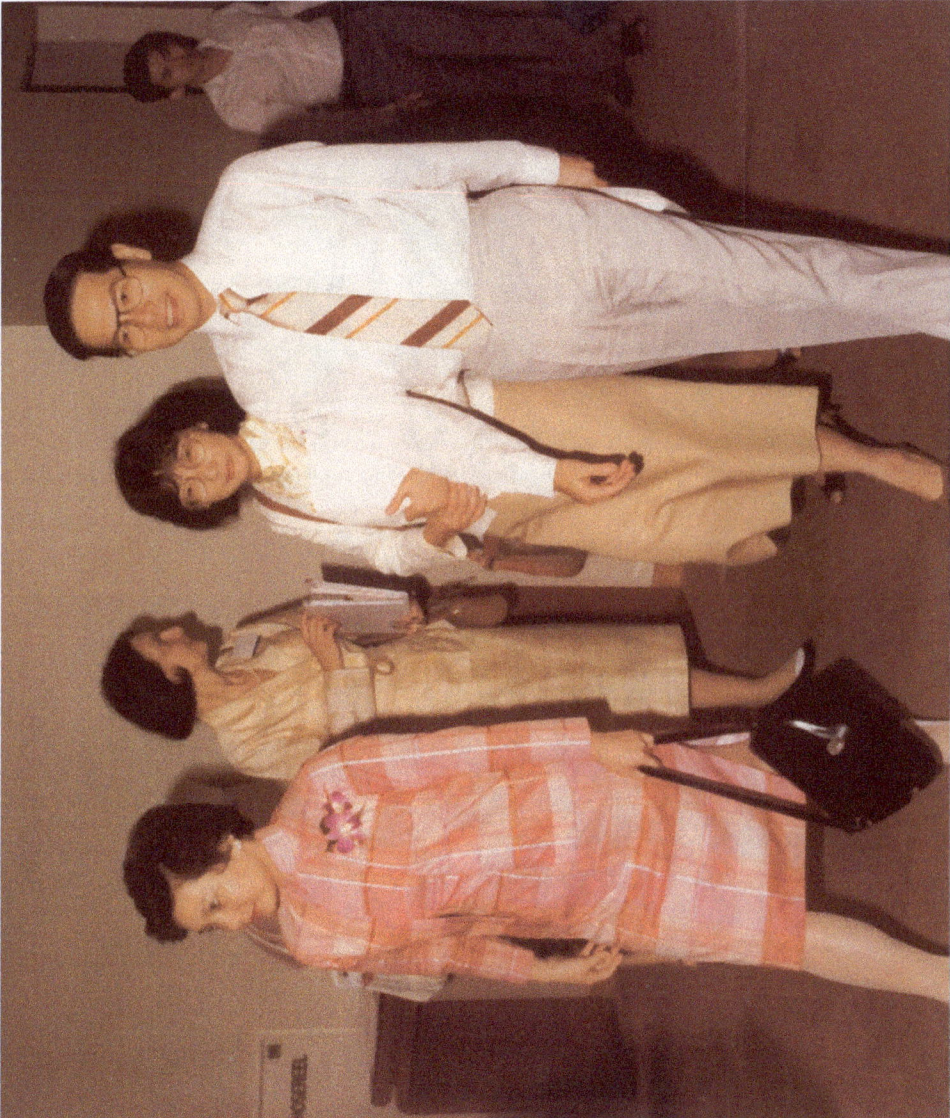

UNICEF-supported event on Early Childhood Development (circa 1986, from right to left). Then Secretary-General of the National Trades Union Congress (NTUC) Ong Teng Cheong, Dr Khoo Kim Choo, UNICEF staff Helen Argyriades and Mrs Yu-Foo Yee Shoon, then Chairman of NTUC Childcare Committee.
Credit: Khoo Kim Choo

Curious Vietnamese children checking out a UNICEF official vehicle in a rural province in northern Vietnam (1994). Credit: Peggy Kek

Penny Whitworth at UNICEF House in New York, 2015.
Credit: Dinia del Sol

The first committee of the newly formed independent Breastfeeding Mothers' Support Group with some of their breastfed children in Singapore in 1991. Lynette Thomas is in the back row, second from right.

Lynette Thomas (back row, in blue patterned shirt) with other members of the Breastfeeding Mothers' Support Group and their children selling delicious food for a fundraiser in Singapore.

UNICEF Singapore staff with an intern (circa 1992).
L–R: Edward Pang, Peggy Kek, intern Connie Hybsier, Penny Whitworth, Sue Oei and Cynthia Ang.

In 1949, a seven-year-old Czech girl, Jitka Samkova, painted a "Thank You" picture for UNICEF help given to her village. It became the first UNICEF greeting card. Credit: Jitka Samkova © UNICEF

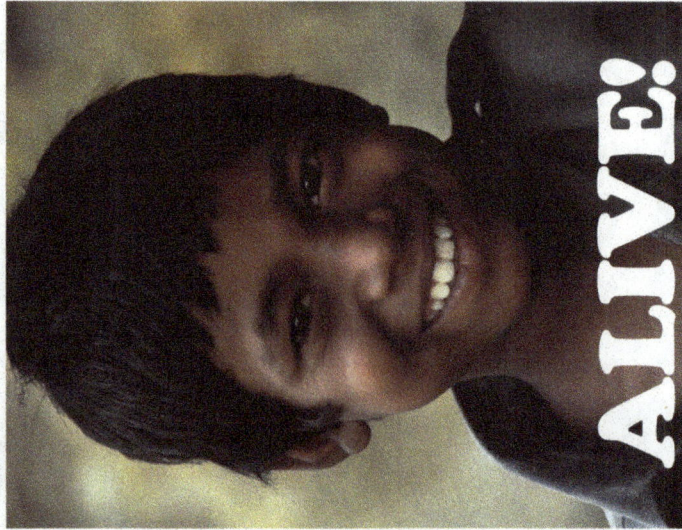

The ALIVE posters were widely used by UNICEF in the 1980s to support the drive to save the lives of millions of children each year based on four simple, low-cost techniques: growth monitoring, oral rehydration therapy, breastfeeding and immunisation, the so-called Child Survival and Development Revolution. Credit: UNICEF

What Would You Like to be When You Grow Up?

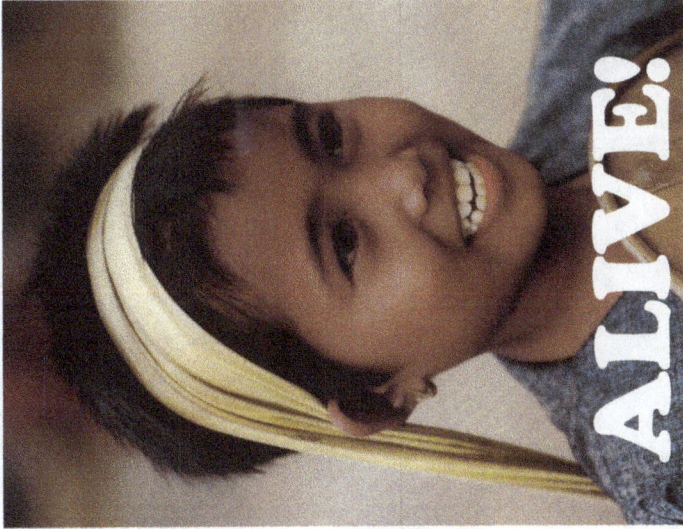

ALIVE!

Breast-milk is the most nutritious food for infants in any country, but in the developing world its advantages over formula feeding can mean the difference between life and death. Breast-milk contains antibodies which protect babies against fatal diarrhoeal diseases; bottle feeding increases the risk of infection. UNICEF, the United Nation's Children's Fund, seeks various ways to protect and promote the practice of breastfeeding.

unicef

What Would You Like to be When You Grow Up?

ALIVE!

More than 12,000 children die each day from diarrhoeal diseases, the biggest single cause of death among the developing world's children. Two-thirds of these deaths result from dehydration and could be prevented by teaching parents how to prepare simple home remedies, such as fluids containing a little salt, plus starchy vegetables or cereals or some kind of sugar.

unicef

The ALIVE posters were were widely used by UNICEF in the 1980s to support the drive to save the lives of millions of children each year based on four simple, low-cost techniques: growth monitoring, oral rehydration therapy, breastfeeding and immunisation, the so-called Child Survival and Development Revolution. Credit: UNICEF

A UNICEF greeting card featuring *The Floating Village* by Singaporean artist Tay Bak Koi.
UNICEF card © UNICEF. Credit: Tay Bak Koi

UNICEF card © UNICEF.
Credit: Tay Bak Koi. Memoirs of Tay Bak Koi, Eagle's Art

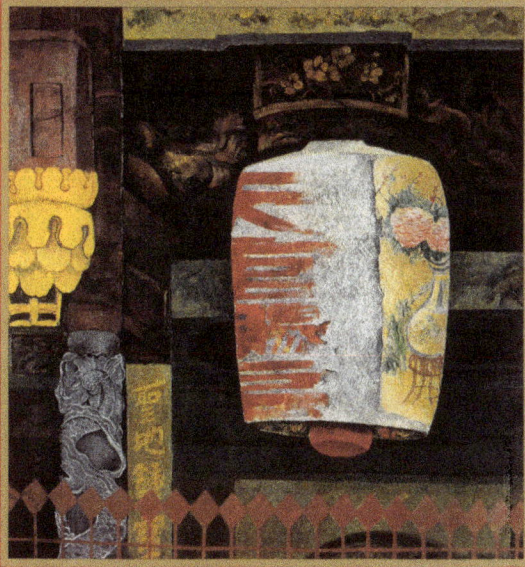

UNICEF card from 1999 featuring *Lantern* by Tay Bak Koi.
© UNICEF. Credit: Tay Bak Koi

Although vaccinations have reduced polio cases by 75 per cent since 1981, the virus still strikes more than 100,000 children every year. UNICEF is supporting programmes to eradicate the disease by the year 2000.

Bien que la vaccination ait réduit de 75 pour cent, depuis 1981, les cas de polio, le virus frappe encore plus de 100 000 enfants chaque année. L'UNICEF soutient des programmes visant à éliminer la maladie d'ici l'an 2000.

Aunque la vacunación ha reducido el número de casos de poliomielitis en 75 por ciento desde 1981, el virus todavía ataca a más de 100.000 niños todos los años. UNICEF apoya los programas a fin de erradicar esta enfermedad para el año 2000.

Tay Bak Koi ★ Singapore • Singapour • Singapur ★ Lantern • Lanterne • Farol.

For the well-being of the world's children ★ Pour le bien-être des enfants du monde ★ Por el bienestar de los niños del mundo ★ На благо всех детей мира ★ 造福世界儿童 ★ لخير ورفاهـة أطفـال العـالم ★

unicef ⓾

United Nations Children's Fund
Fonds des Nations Unies pour l'enfance

99H74 / 0838-Y
recycled paper/papier recyclé

Printed in Canada/Imprimé au Canada

The back of the card features an informational message.
© UNICEF. Credit: Tay Bak Koi

The late Tay Bak Koi posing in front of one of his own paintings in 1997.
Credit: Joy Loh

Lee Hock Moh with Peggy Kek in front of his painting, *Glowing*, in 2015.
Credit: Lee Hock Moh and Art Tree Gallery.

The artist, Yong Cheong Thye in 2015.
Credit: Kanti Bajpai

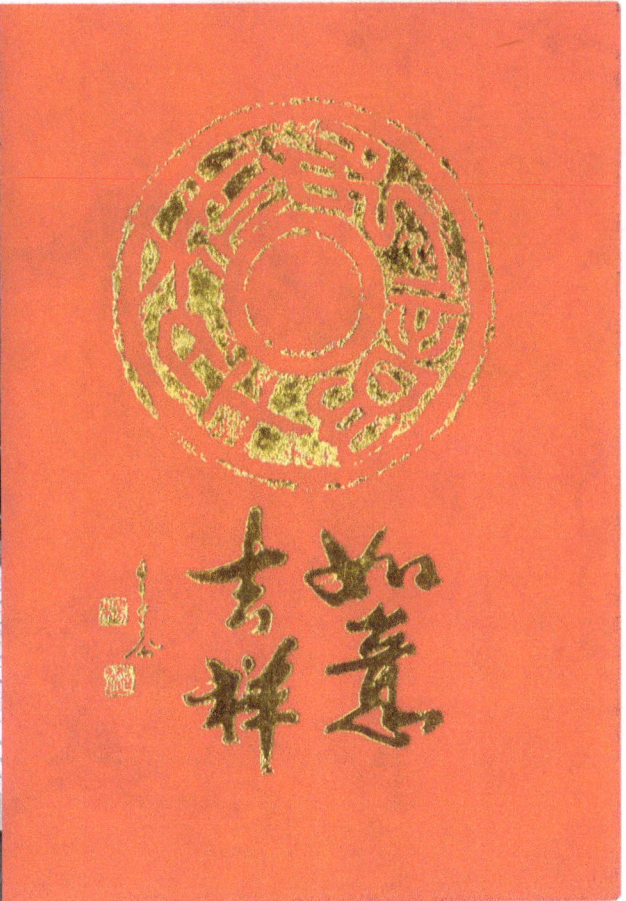

UNICEF greeting card from 1993 featuring *Good Fortune* by Yong Cheong Thye. © UNICEF.
Credit: Yong Cheong Thye

UNICEF greeting card from 1994 featuring *May Your Wishes Come True* by Yong Cheong Thye.
© UNICEF. Credit: Yong Cheong Thye

UNICEF stationery set from 1986 and greeting card from 1992 featuring *Glowing* by Lee Hock Moh.
© UNICEF. Credit: Lee Hock Moh and Art Tree Gallery

United Nations Children's Fund
Fonds des Nations Unies pour l'enfance
Fondo de las Naciones Unidas para la Infancia

Greeting Card Operation
360 Orchard Road #05-01B
International Building
Singapore 0923
Tel: 737-6079
Telex: RS 39609 UNICEF
Fax: (65) 732-8824

unicef

29 October 1991

Mdn Chang Hoei, Christine
20 Cheow Keng Road
Singapore 1542

Dear Mdn Chang,

I have recently arrived in Singapore as the Manager of the UNICEF Greeting Card Operation here.

One of my objectives is to promote greater awareness of UNICEF, the United Nations Children's Fund, and to increase the number of opportunities for people in Singapore to participate in its work.

As you know UNICEF, the United Nations Children's Fund relies on voluntary contribution from governments and individuals to assist the millions of children in 128 developing countries whose basic rights to adequate nutrition, health care and education remain unfulfilled. An important part of UNICEF's annual revenue is raised through the sale of cards and other products. Last year alone, sales provided nearly US$60 million towards UNICEF programmes.

One of the most important voluntary contribution to UNICEF is that of artists and museums around the world who donate the reproduction rights of their works for UNICEF cards and products.

Last Monday I attended the opening ceremony of the Singapore Multi Media Art Exhibition '91. I saw your works and thought that they (or others) may be suitable as UNICEF cards.

If you would be interested in submitting a work I would be very pleased to meet with you to discuss details with you. I enclose for your information a set of guidelines for submission of artworks.

I look forward to hearing from you.

Yours sincerely,

Penny Whitworth
Manager

UNICEF letter 1991. Credit: Cristene Chang

---

unicef

United Nations Children's Fund
Fonds des Nations Unies pour l'enfance
Fondo de las Naciones Unidas para la Infancia

Greeting Card Operation
360 Orchard Road #05-01B
International Building
Singapore 0923
Tel: 737-6079
Telex: RS 39609 UNICEF
Fax: (65) 732-8824

9 December 1993

Yong Cheong Thye
Yong Gallery
No 17 Erskine Road
Singapore 0106

Dear Mr Yong,

Artists for the Children of the World

In recognition of the artists around the world who have contributed their art works to UNICEF for reproduction as greeting cards, UNICEF has developed a special exhibit celebrating this very privileged partnership that we enjoy.

The retrospective pays hommage to the diversity of talent which has been dedicated to the world's children since the 1950s. Singaporean artists have been well represented over the years.

An Exhibition will take place at The Hyatt Regency Singapore from 14-16 January 1993. In this way we will publicly thank you and the other Singaporean artists for their contribution to fundraising for UNICEF programmes.

On this occasion we would also like to invite you to display 3-4 original works alongside the panels and cards. We would be delighted if you would accept to do so.

Professor Tommy Koh has graciously accepted to officially open this exhibition at 10am on 14 January 1994. I would like to invite you to be present at this very special occasion.

Thank you for your kind consideration of this request.

Yours sincerely,

Penny Whitworth
Manager

UNICEF letter 1993. Credit: Yong Cheong Thye

Top: The artist, Cristene Chang.
Credit: Cristene Chang

Left: UNICEF greeting card
from 1994 featuring *Joyful
Abundance* by Cristene Chang.
© UNICEF.
Credit: Cristene Chang

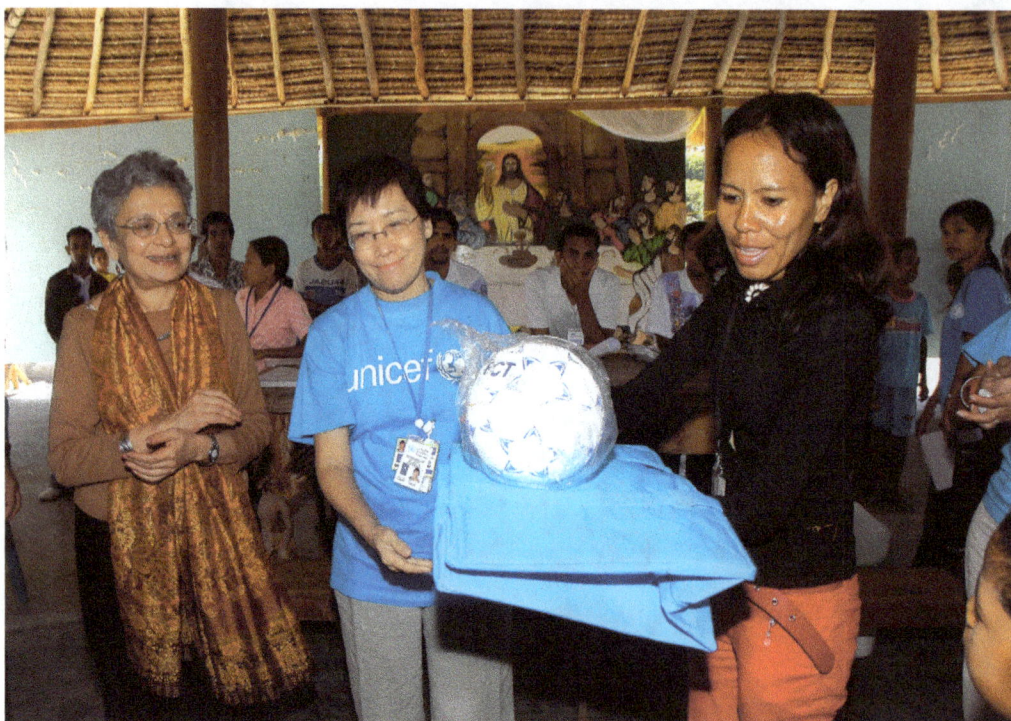

UNICEF Regional Director Anupama Rao Singh (far left) and Timor Leste Representative Dr Ng Shui-Meng hand over recreational kits to Liquica Emergency Commission Coordinator Maria Natalia.
Credit: UNICEF Timor-Leste/ 2006/ Lay

UNICEF Timor Leste Representative Dr Ng Shui-Meng playing with a little girl at a Dili district police station. The police station is opening its new office for Vulnerable Persons Unit (VPU).
Credit: UNICEF Timor-Leste/2007/Setyanto

Regional Fundraising Workshop in Manila (1997) where participants visited a UNICEF-sponsored project. Jackie Leung (second from left in back row, in white) is next to Eduard Spescha on her left and Penny Whitworth on her right.

Cheng Wing-Sie (third from right) with a group of health officials at a rural health centre in Yunnan, China (2008).

Cheng Wing-Sie with a group of district health staff in rural Mandalay, Myanmar. On the far right is Dr Khun Ohmar Sann, then Director, National AIDS/STI Programme in Myanmar.

Cheng Wing-Sie (second from left) in Beijing with senior staff of the National Health and Family Planning Commission of the People's Republic of China (2015).

Peggy Kek with pupils of a UNICEF–assisted school in northern Vietnam (1994).

Dr Vivian Balakrishnan, Minister for Community Development, Youth and Sports at a conference held in Singapore in 2009 to examine the impact of the economic crisis on children.
Credit: Lee Kuan Yew School of Public Policy, National University of Singapore

Indonesian Finance Minister, Sri Mulyani with UNICEF Regional Director for East Asia and Pacific, Anupama Rao Singh at the same conference.
Credit: Lee Kuan Yew School of Public Policy, National University of Singapore

Section 3

Volunteer Action in Singapore

Civil Society: A Special Relationship

Penny Whitworth

Penny Whitworth writes of the energy and dedication of individual volunteers and organisations, who have conveyed the appeal of UNICEF and children to so many and with astounding results. They make invaluable contributions and augment UNICEF's efforts to ensure health, education, equality and protection for every child.

UNICEF is not funded from the UN budget. It is funded exclusively by voluntary contributions from governmental and non-governmental sources. Approximately a third of its funds is raised from individual donors, corporations and civil society organisations worldwide that are strongly committed to UNICEF's work.

Many people in industrialised countries first hear about UNICEF's work through the activities of 36 National Committees for UNICEF. These non-governmental organisations serve as the public face and dedicated voice of UNICEF; they are a unique feature of UNICEF's global organisation. They work tirelessly to raise funds from the private sector, create key corporate and civil society partnerships, promote children's rights and secure worldwide visibility for children threatened by poverty, disasters, armed conflict, abuse and exploitation. Beyond this, they promote public awareness and the fulfilment of child rights in their respective countries. They also rally many different partners — including the media, national and local government officials, NGOs, specialists such as doctors and lawyers, corporations, schools, young people and the general public — on issues relating to children's rights.

During the early years of UNICEF's existence, talented individuals were inspired to volunteer their time and their mobilising power to help the cause of improving children's survival and well-being worldwide. Possibly the best known of these early advocates was Danny Kaye, a famous US actor and comedian. In 1954 he became UNICEF's first "Ambassador-at-Large", spreading the message about the situation of children, their needs and the opportunity to help, around the world. He subsequently made a 20-minute documentary film, *Assignment Children*, that was seen by more than 100 million people, making UNICEF a household name worldwide. Many others have followed in Danny Kaye's footsteps over the years, and continue to do so, becoming Goodwill Ambassadors for UNICEF.

> *I believe deeply that children are more powerful than oil, more beautiful than rivers, more precious than any other natural resource a country can have... I feel that the most rewarding thing I have ever done in my life is to be associated with UNICEF.*

> Danny Kaye, UNICEF's first "Ambassador-at-Large"

Kaye's optimism about the future of the world's children, and his conviction of the vital role UNICEF could play in that future, never flagged. "The goals of the child health revolution can be reached," he said in a statement to UNICEF's Executive Board in 1983. "However discouraging it may look at any given time, it can be done when people of goodwill band together and strive for the best. UNICEF's work is a tribute to mankind and to the superior will of man."[1]

In October 1971 Mr Kaye visited Singapore on a UNICEF mission to film school health services in South-East Asia as part of a TV documentary recording the relevance and impact of UNICEF's work for 25 years. True to form, he went straight from the airport to a primary school to meet the children. He watched them brushing their teeth as the film crew recorded. They also filmed a government-sponsored crèche for working parents.

In Singapore, as in other places, people I met were keen to know more about the situation of children elsewhere, how UNICEF worked to improve their lives and prospects and what they could do to contribute. They came from all walks of life and professional activity, volunteering in their spare time after work or class and over the weekends. Some took initiatives of their own and organised independent activities, others joined existing programmes. The majority of their action revolved around the sale of UNICEF cards, even before there was a local office.

---

[1] For more information on UNICEF Ambassadors, including Danny Kaye, visit http://www.unicef.org/about/history/index_celebrities.html

Before the establishment of the UNICEF Office, it was the Singapore Council of Social Service, or SCCS (known today as the National Council of Social Service) that was responsible for the sale of UNICEF cards in Singapore. The Singapore Junior Chamber of Commerce[2] (or Jaycees) sold UNICEF cards for several years under the auspices of the SCCS. In those days there was a direct association that could be reported to consumers between the sale of cards and the benefits. In 1960 UNICEF provided more than one million pounds of milk powder through government welfare centres. In 1961 UNICEF contributed to mass x-ray campaigns conducted in Singapore to combat tuberculosis, and provided facilities and milk for children in need and for their mothers.

In 1960, 2,000 Boy Scouts from 160 troops sold UNICEF greeting cards door to door in a campaign organised by the Jaycees. Over 10,000 cards were sold with the Pasir Panjang Secondary School Scout Group responsible for one quarter of those sales.

During the 1980s and 1990s, when there was a UNICEF office in Singapore, sales stands were organised in shopping centres, at places of work, social gatherings and cultural institutions. These could not have been operated without volunteer assistance. As UNICEF was a relatively unknown entity for many passers-by, running a sales booth was often as much about informing people about children at risk and what UNICEF was doing to help, as helping customers to choose cards and gifts. Sales volunteers also needed to be fit, as they do all round the world, as often the booths were what we would call today "pop-ups" with tables, decoration, information materials and products being taken to the site, set up, and then dismantled at the end of the day. Before this, volunteers would come to the office to help prepare the items to be taken to the sales booths; at the height of the holiday preparations, this could mean sales stands in several different locations on the same day.

One of the most memorable activities for me was a collection of newspapers and clothes organised by students of the Social Welfare Club at Nanyang Technological University (NTU) in 1992. Their planning and execution were flawless. It was a complex, collaborative operation requiring multiple authorisations including the Ministry of Environment, meticulous logistical arrangements with a fleet of trucks and perfect teamwork. Flyers were distributed in advance to alert residents of what would be collected on that Sunday, why it was being collected, how it would be

---

[2] The Jaycees, called JCI today, is a long-time UNICEF partner. In 2015, the non-profit organisation celebrates 100 years of young active citizens committed to finding sustainable solutions for community problems with active participation in the United Nations.

collected and its final destination. Over 200 tonnes were collected by nearly 1,500 students raising over $38,000 in just one day. At that time it was the largest-ever collection and the largest-ever single donation to UNICEF in Singapore. The funds were used for education and health projects in Mozambique. I worked with the students throughout the preparations and on the day itself. Very quickly I gained a tremendous respect for their dedication, resourcefulness, professionalism, precision and solidarity. Evidence of the benefits of military training undergone by a number of the project leaders was obvious. I learned a lot during that time, not least on the day itself as we hurried up and down and across the floors of HDB estates and communities eager to meet the ambitious goals the students had set. Everyone involved, including residents, was keen to make a success of the event. The response, goodwill and generosity will stay with me forever.

In 1993, in response to the enthusiastic response to talks given in schools and the high levels of curiosity from the school children about how their contemporaries in other countries lived, the UNICEF office organised a series of storytelling sessions in the Central and Branch Libraries. The storytelling sessions provided an excellent and enjoyable educational opportunity, increasing global awareness and understanding. Most of the sessions were run by volunteers, some of whom were primary school teachers. They picked their own stories and planned the activities that followed the storytelling. Children between the ages of six and 12 were told about how youngsters elsewhere lived, played and, in some cases, worked. They asked questions and talked about what they had learned, did some role-playing exercises and made drawings. A UNICEF staff member who conducted one of the sessions at the Queenstown Library remembers it as a highlight of her career with the organisation.

Another terrific example in the pattern of young people taking on board an issue that troubled them and doing something to make a difference took place in 1993 when the United Nations Students Association at the National University of Singapore learned about the high numbers of children in Nepal who died as a result of diarrhoeal diseases, often dehydration. Acute diarrhoea still accounts for nearly 1.3 million deaths a year worldwide among children under five years of age, making it the second most common cause of child deaths worldwide. Two recent advances in managing diarrhoeal disease — newly formulated oral rehydration salts (ORS) containing lower concentrations of glucose and salt, and zinc supplementation as part of the treatment and rotavirus vaccines — can drastically reduce the number of child deaths. These new methods, used in addition to prevention and treatment with appropriate fluids, breastfeeding, continued feeding and selective use of antibiotics will reduce the duration and severity of diarrhoeal episodes and lower their incidence.[3]

The students organised a weekend carnival to raise awareness and funds for UNICEF-assisted programmes in Nepal. There were performances, including a Spanish dance in costume, and a newspaper collection in two housing estates.

Collectively, these voluntary efforts and those recounted by others in this book serve as a gentle reminder that no matter what skills we possess or experience we have, they can be put to good use to play a meaningful role in making the world a better place for children. The pleasure and satisfaction in participating and contributing, making a difference, is a universal response. For some reason, it is a surprise each time we encounter this in our lives. Editing this book has rekindled lifelong friendships that were formed around many of these activities.

---

[3] For more information on such acute diarrhoeal disease, visit http://www.unicef.org/health/index_43834.html

Not All Business

Tony Coker

Born in the UK in 1966 to Nigerian parents, Tony Coker has two brothers and a sister and spent his childhood in Sunbury-on-Thames with a British foster family. Tony left school at 16 to start working and feels fortunate to have worked for international companies, where he obtained training and experience in different countries that enabled him eventually to set up his own airfreight forwarding company. He currently specialises in transportation solutions in West and Central Africa.

After four years of living in Los Angeles, California, my employer offered me the chance to be posted to Singapore in 1992. It was a place I knew nothing of, but was attracted to initially because it was a country located in Asia, a part of the world to which I had never travelled before. I felt this opportunity, to experience a new culture and increase my knowledge and experience in my field of work, would be enriching.

I remember arriving at Changi Airport in October 1992 and wondering the purpose of the continuous ringing sound inside the taxi that was transporting me to my hotel. Eventually I found out it was to alert the driver whenever he went over the speed limit. I arrived in Singapore on a Friday and was looking forward to a rest over the weekend. This was soon shattered when, at 8.30am, my hotel phone rang and I was given my welcome to Singapore. "Morning, Tony, it's Steven, I am at the reception waiting to take you to the office." Half-day Saturdays were previously unknown to me.

Being English-born and educated, I had no difficulty with language, although as my first weeks passed, I became slightly apprehensive about the limited number of African people in Singapore at that time (that I was aware of) and I wondered whether I would face any resistance or non-acceptance.

Only to my later knowledge do I recollect how fast this apprehension dissolved, as the warmth of the welcome I felt from many Singaporeans both in business and outside began to touch me. I found that as much as I might have been curious about Singaporeans, they were also curious about me. Meeting people and establishing relationships was not difficult and this really contributed to my feeling comfortable and at ease.

Sometime in 1993 on one of my visits back to Los Angeles, I remember walking into a store off Venice Beach and seeing these cool rubber bags and eye-catching bottle cap belts, all made from recycled materials. These were made by a small two-man company in southern US called Recycle Revolution. I loved the uniqueness of what I saw and on the spot bought myself a belt. On the plane back to Singapore, I began thinking about how these could be brought to Singapore as a way of introducing creative ways to recycle.

I had been thinking about how selling these products would not only have a positive impact on waste reduction but also about how I could combine this with a social cause. In 1994 the idea of recycling was not widely circulating in Singapore. The idea of using recycled goods for fashion accessories was even less prevalent. So Recycle World was born in Singapore, a company with the simple aim to increase the awareness of Singaporeans of the possible uses of recycled materials in fashion accessories.

My first encounter with UNICEF Singapore was to present Recycle World Pte Ltd and our desire to contribute a percentage of income from the sales of our products to UNICEF Singapore. I was graciously welcomed by Penny Whitworth and Peggy Kek who attentively listened to my introduction. Many ideas were shared and the beginning of a relationship built.

Recycle World began introducing into the Singapore fashion market, a range of bags made from recycled car parts, business card holders made from computer mother boards, earrings and many other unique and funky accessories. The manufacturers from the United States would scour car dumps and collect seatbelts, seatbelt buckles, rubber tyres and number plates, which would be cleaned, treated and cut into bags. All the items would be hand-made in the small workshop of Recycle Revolution in Kansas. These items were sold in Singapore, in places such as departmental store CK Tang and other boutique shops.

We chose to approach UNICEF because of the connection we found between the youth our products were attracting and the youth UNICEF were impacting. My knowledge of UNICEF came years earlier when my mum would buy UNICEF Christmas cards. After that I learnt more about the health improvement goals and other admirable work that UNICEF had been doing around the world for many years. Buying a Recycle World product was a very simple way of sensitising the purchaser of the fact that they were contributing towards the well-being of other children in developing countries. Our hope was that this would stimulate them to see how they could participate in other ways and contribute towards the work of UNICEF Singapore.

Many years later, I was once again involved in the work of another humanitarian organisation, this time in Africa during the Ebola outbreak in early 2014. My Europe-based freight company was directly engaged in the efforts of the NGO Médecins Sans Frontières (also known as Doctors Without Borders) when we were contracted to transport relief goods for their difficult assignment in Ebola-affected areas. These included medicines, personal protective wear and generators. Some of the medical supplies had to be transported under stringent temperature control, and there were strict instructions to expedite the passage of the goods and get them cleared swiftly through customs with duty-free exemptions. Goods were delivered by chartered as well as commercial aircraft, and sometimes by sea if they could not fit into an aircraft. Some of the towns we delivered to were Kailahun, one of the Sierra Leone's first hotspots during the outbreak, as well as Magburaka, Bo and Makeni, also in Sierra Leone.

After almost five years in Singapore, I found my Singapore beauty; her name is Vindy. We married and very soon after, we left to return to England. We remained in England for a year and then due to a work posting, we moved to Brussels in Belgium. We now live in Brussels with our five children but often visit family and friends who remain in Singapore.

Breastfeeding Mothers' Support Group (Singapore) and UNICEF

Lynette Thomas

Lynette Thomas spent 24 years with the Breastfeeding Mothers' Support Group (Singapore), BMSG. She joined the group when her first child was one year old. She became a Life Member of BMSG and served on the Committee for 12 years where she was also a Breastfeeding Counsellor. Her roles also included serving as Editor of the BMSG newsletter called Keeping Abreast, *Librarian, Secretary and President for two terms from 1991. In 1999 she received a Long Service Award from Singapore's Ministry of Community Development "in recognition of 10 years of invaluable voluntary service to the community".*

At the heart of every breastfeeding mothers' support group is a desire to provide mother-to-mother support and assistance to new mothers wishing to breastfeed their babies. In Singapore in the decades of the latter half of the 20th century, as in many countries around the world, the prevalence of formula feeding thanks to uncontrolled and aggressive marketing of such substitutes meant that women no longer had access to traditional wisdom and knowledge about breastfeeding among their peers and from their own mothers' generation.

The rates of women breastfeeding and continuing to breastfeed well into their child's first year were lamentably low, and unfortunately it was common for formula feeding to be encouraged from the time of the hospital stay, with mothers being sent home with a free tin of whichever formula was being promoted that month. Hospital staff had perhaps as little as a one-hour lecture on breastfeeding in their entire training and, not being conversant with how to support mothers who wished to breastfeed, hospitals often instituted practices that effectively made breastfeeding almost impossible. Separating mothers and their babies was routine, ensuring skin-to-skin contact immediately after birth unheard of, and feeding "by the clock" was the normal practice. This meant that even though the established wisdom was that "breast is best", hospitals and their staff were contributing to the demise of breastfeeding.

The global decline in breastfeeding set alarm bells ringing, and in the 1970s groups began to form to halt this decline and a number of voluntary organisations provided peer support to mothers and advocated against the formula companies and their rampant marketing campaigns. The Breastfeeding Mothers' Support Group (BMSG) was formed in 1975 and immediately set out to do the same. From the start it received the assistance of some key medical personnel including Professor Wong Hock Boon, Professor Maureen Tsakok, Dr Dixie Tan (who became the patron of the group), Dr Noel Leong and others.

Initially, BMSG operated with the support of the National Council for Social Service (NCSS). In 1991 it became an independent, non-profit society and was granted a tax-exempt status under the Ministry of Health's Health Endowment Fund in 1997. BMSG came under the umbrella of the Singapore Council of Women's Organisations (SCWO) soon after and took up office space there around 1997 after having had a storage space and telephone answering machine at the Family Life Services (a catholic organisation) for about a decade.

The aims of the BMSG were twofold: to provide peer support through trained breastfeeding counsellors and to promote and encourage breastfeeding throughout the country. Already established support groups in other countries, such as the then Nursing Mothers' Association of Australia, were invaluable in providing materials for the promotion of breastfeeding among expectant mothers and the proper training of breastfeeding counsellors. A telephone counselling service was set up and regular public talks to expectant couples were held across the island.

In line with the World Health Organization (WHO) recommendations for mothers to breastfeed exclusively for the first six months and, with supplementary nutrition from solid food, well into the second year of a child's life, the BMSG promoted this as the best outcome to achieve. However, recognising that many women opted to return to work immediately following their two months' maternity leave, the Group also ensured that this would not be a hindrance to mothers who were breastfeeding. The talks included information on how mothers could keep up their milk supply so that the baby could receive expressed breast milk during the day and were able to feed directly when the mother was at home.

Alongside its efforts to support mothers in their decision and efforts to breast-feed, the Group's members also advocated best practices in hospitals and among medical staff. From its early days volunteers delivered seminars to the nurses and doctors of hospital maternity wards to enhance their knowledge and understanding of how mothers could be supported to breastfeed in hospital and encouraged to continue after their discharge.

So in 1991, when UNICEF and WHO began the Baby Friendly Health Initiative, the BMSG threw its full support behind it. The Group actively promoted the 10 steps that hospitals were required to follow to be deemed a Baby Friendly Hospital. These included practical measures such as having a rooming-in policy, helping mothers initiate breastfeeding within half an hour of birth and ensuring new-born infants were not given fluids other than breast milk unless medically indicated.

On May 22, 1992, Janet Nelson, UNICEF's Chief Non-Government Liaison, visited Singapore with a view to meeting non-governmental organisations such as BMSG as well as the few lactation consultants practising at the time. Her visit was followed by the visit of Richard Reid, UNICEF's Director of Public Affairs, on October 27, 1992 who met with UNICEF's Greeting Card Operation Manager in Singapore Penny Whitworth and three committee members of BMSG to discuss the Baby Friendly Hospital Initiative. It was hoped that his discussions with the Ministry of Health would be an impetus for greater action in the promotion of breastfeeding. Subsequently, the Obstetrics and Gynaecology Society in Singapore expressed its intention to organise a public forum with UNICEF in early 1993.

At this time too, the World Alliance for Breastfeeding Action (WABA) with support from UNICEF and the WHO launched the first World Breastfeeding Week in August 1992. BMSG was enthusiastic in its support of this new initiative to garner support for breastfeeding in the community, and has celebrated the week every year since, with various activities including talks by world-renowned experts in breastfeeding.

In tandem with these efforts, the Group has worked with the Sale of Infant Foods Ethics Committee Singapore (SIFECS) to ensure that milk formula companies complied with its Code's accepted marketing practices for their products. SIFECS was set up in 1979 by the Ministry of Health, and undertook several revisions to its Code to bring it into closer alignment with the WHO's International Code of Marketing of Breast Milk Substitutes that was introduced in 1981. The BMSG has always had a member on the board of SIFECS and regularly vets marketing materials to ensure there are no violations. Despite the SIFECS Code not being fully aligned with the WHO Code (it only covers the marketing of milk formula up to six months of age) it was seen as prudent to work within what was in place.

Around 1991, the International Baby Food Action Network (IBFAN) also contacted BMSG to seek the Group's help to put pressure on government and private hospitals to ban the donation of free samples of infant formula to mothers, to ensure infant formula was not marketed inappropriately. The ban was finally included in the SIFECS Code in 2010. IBFAN also supported the Group in continuing to work closely with the Ministry of Health to encourage and support more initiatives to promote and support a breastfeeding culture in Singapore.

Without the overarching efforts of WHO, UNICEF, WABA and IBFAN; the contributions of the medical profession and their administrators; and the impassioned volunteerism of breastfeeding mothers' support groups all working together to promote and support breastfeeding, we would not be seeing the steady rise in breastfeeding that has taken place in the past 20 years.

According to Singapore's National Breastfeeding Survey in 2001, where 2,098 local mothers were interviewed at two and six months post-partum, 94.5% had initiated breastfeeding. At two months, 49.6% were still breastfeeding, and at six months 21.1% (non-exclusively). In 2011, 1,962 mothers were interviewed for the same survey, and 99% had initiated breastfeeding. At two months, 80% were still breastfeeding (28% exclusively) and 42% were still breastfeeding at six months (1% exclusively).

While there is still much to be done, it is heartening to see in 2015 that there are now three Baby Friendly Hospitals in Singapore — the National University Hospital, the Singapore General Hospital and the KK Women's & Children's Hospital. At the time of writing, two other private hospitals are working to implement the 10 steps that will enable them to gain accreditation in the near future.

While the hospital environment is crucial in helping mothers begin to establish breastfeeding, it is interesting that the 10th step in UNICEF's set of guidelines emphasises the vital role that mother-to-mother support has in ensuring the continuation of breastfeeding once the mother is at home. It is to "foster the establishment of breastfeeding support groups and refer mothers to them upon discharge from the hospital or clinic."

This one-to-one support is often what is most needed and most appreciated by new mothers. It is the modern-day equivalent of village members coming to help the new mother and her baby. It is what every breastfeeding mothers' support group regards as its duty and wholehearted desire.

Miracle on 34th Street:
UNICEF and Dreams Coming True

Kenneth Tan

Kenneth Tan is Chairman of the Singapore Film Society. He has more than 30 years'
experience in broadcasting, cinema operations and movie distribution. Twenty years ago,
his love of film led him to work on one of UNICEF's largest charity film screenings in
Singapore at the time, which in turn led him to his dream job.

Like many people, I used to have what I would call only "generic awareness" of
UNICEF. I knew broadly of its humanitarian agendas. I'd received UNICEF greeting cards over the years from people otherwise unrelated to the organisation. But
I had never had personal contact with or in-depth knowledge of UNICEF itself or
its specific work. All this changed in 1994. My life changed. Literally.

As a backdrop for appreciating exactly how profound and moving my interface
with UNICEF was to become, I should first describe what I do and how what I'm
chronicling in this essay came about.

I have spent all my adult life in the film and television industry. I started going
to the cinema on my own at the age of 11. I first pressed the changeover button
on a theatrical motion picture projector when I was 13. I got elected as Chairman
of our national cinema organisation (the Singapore Film Society, or SFS for short)
before I commemorated my crossing of the age-of-majority threshold, taking over
from a predecessor almost thrice my physical age. Today, more than three decades
later, I still chair SFS, having since been at the helm of our nationwide terrestrial
broadcaster MediaCorp as well as Singapore's largest cinema chain Golden
Village.

Unplanned and unanticipated, UNICEF was to play an instrumental role in landing me that dream job of running Golden Village.

It was in early 1994 when I became aware of the then-upcoming remake of the classic Christmas film, *Miracle on 34th Street*, about a department store Santa Claus who moves the heart of a cynical child and brings renewed warmth and love into her family and the lives of those around them. Veteran actor Richard Attenborough was to play the lead role of Kris Kringle. Major Hollywood studio 20th Century Fox was the producer and worldwide distributor.

This kind of advance information about new movies was and is *de rigeur* in my line of work. More than many industry practitioners, I've always taken a deep personal interest in films, beyond noting the key parameters that can become potential "hooks" for marketing campaigns when the movie opens in my cinemas. I had watched the original *Miracle on 34th Street* as a child. I was curious to see how the remake would turn out.

Because of that film, UNICEF came into my life, through Peggy Kek.

Peggy not only inducted me into the world of UNICEF. She took that *Miracle* movie and transformed it into a real-life miracle in my own life. The chain of events that she and UNICEF set in motion transformed me forever.

Peggy was working for UNICEF Singapore at that time, and got in touch with me about the new film, in early 1994. What she wanted to explore was the possibility of tying up with the year-end release of the film in local cinemas, to do a fundraising and/or awareness-generating event in support of UNICEF's Greeting Card Operation in Singapore.

I vividly remember my spontaneous response to Peggy. It should not be difficult to do, I felt and said. Fox (as we industry folks always referred to 20th Century Fox in abbreviation) held the rights to the film. We'd need to get their blessing, and find a suitable venue — then organise the event ideally before the public release of the film.

I had the Fox office phone number in memory — not the phone book of today's smartphones; my personal memory. Merely because I talked to Fox almost every week. I rang Singapore Managing Director John Foo, who said, sure, go ahead, Fox was already aware of Richard Attenborough's status as UNICEF Goodwill Ambassador and would be glad to help.

Next, I brought Peggy, UNICEF Manager Penny Whitworth (who was head of the UNICEF Singapore office), and Golden Village CEO David Glass together for a preliminary meeting. Golden Village was a new player in the Singapore cinema market at that time, having built and opened Asia's first multiplex (multi-screen cinema complex) in 1992. I had briefed Peggy and Penny to expect to have to pay for the use of the film and the venue, and to have to go along with the cinema operator's specification of availability of space and date(s).

David was incredibly warm, welcoming, empathetic and enthusiastic. He agreed on the spot to our arbitrarily suggested date, 8th December. We chose the biggest hall at Golden Village's Yishun 10 multiplex (the 416-seater, as we wanted to be able to sell the maximum number of tickets to raise funds). He instantly said yes, without even checking what other movies Golden Village might have to displace to make room for UNICEF.

And he refused to allow us to pay anything for that.

Peggy and Penny were bowled over by the generosity of Golden Village and Fox. So was I. We profusely thanked David, and then embarked on our months of planning and preparation.

We invited Nominated Member of Parliament, orthopaedic surgeon and well-known advocate for women, Dr Kanwaljit Soin[1], to be our Guest-of-Honour for the evening.

We imposed repeatedly on Golden Village, to get foyer space for exhibition of UNICEF's greeting cards and collaterals; to access the cinema for advance testing of film and equipment; for coordination of ticketing and marketing material and a plethora of other needs. We spent so much time with and at Golden Village that we (and they) joked about giving us desks of our own.

The ensuing months were hectic, fruitful, insightful and fun. I lost count of the amount of time we spent with each other — not just Peggy and Penny and I, but also our respective UNICEF and SFS teams. We combed through publicity litera-ture and visuals from the film owners. We worked with graphic designers and printers to strike the best balance between creativity and clarity of the marketing material we needed to produce and use. We liaised back and forth with the offices and staff of Dr Soin and Golden Village. We went out and talked to numerous community groups, spreading the word, selling tickets and building many new friendships. By osmosis, I gradually assimilated some of the substance and ethos of UNICEF. I was both humbled and energised by the depth and breadth of UNICEF's work with children, and through their other Goodwill Ambassadors

---

[1] Dr Kanwaljit Soin was the first woman Nominated Member of Parliament in Singapore, and also then, the immediate past president of the women's advocacy group, Association of Women for Action and Research (AWARE). UNICEF invited Dr Soin because the welfare of children is closely tied to the welfare of women, and she was known in Singapore for her tireless work on behalf of women.

who were all global luminaries — Roger Moore and Audrey Hepburn being two of the most striking role models to me. Peggy, Penny and I became firm friends. My respect and admiration for what they, their team and the whole organisation were doing just grew and grew.

I had previously thought that, being neither a doctor nor a trained counsellor, I could never meaningfully contribute to any people-sector entity as a volunteer. The experience of interfacing with UNICEF through these two spunky and dedicated ladies taught me otherwise. I learned that each and every one of us can play a part in a cause like this, whatever our training and domain knowledge may be.

The big night arrived. We had sold almost every seat in the house. Our Guest-of-Honour was due to reach the venue at 7 pm. Our fellow volunteers were there much earlier in the day. I got there at 5.30 pm. The first thing I saw was David, looking dapper and happy as he always is, in a smart suit with polished shoes and matching tie and breast-pocket hanky. All of his Golden Village staff were busy with the final preparations for our premiere.

We received Dr Soin punctually, gave our speeches and started the screening. As the opening credits rolled and we sat with our audience, we relished not only the movie that was unfolding before our eyes, but also the shared appreciation and enjoyment that our full house of well-wishers was experiencing with us.

At the end of the show, the house lights came on, there was loud and sustained applause, and we walked our smiling Guest-of-Honour to her car. As we waved goodbye, I felt that one-of-a-kind sense of accomplishment, elation and emptiness, all at once. We'd made it!! Everything was fine, and done!! And there would be this "void" in my life the next day and for some time to come, without our UNICEF film premiere to think about and prepare for.

It was now 9.40 pm. Some of us had eaten a bit beforehand, but all of us were famished. We spontaneously decided to bring all the volunteers and Golden Village staff who had helped us, out for dinner nearby. And so, also impromptu, we asked David if he'd like to join us. For as long as I live, I shall never, ever, forget what happened next.

At 9.43 pm, on 8th December 1994, in Singapore, at Golden Village Yishun 10.

"Oh thanks, KT, I'd love to, but it's my wife's birthday today, and we pushed back our dinner celebration so I could come and help you make sure everything was okay for your premiere."

Wow.

To say the least, we were touched beyond anything conveyable on a printed page. Had we not thought of dinner and asking David, we would never even have known. Way back when we had first met up with him and named our date, he could have said no and counter-proposed an alternative date. Or he could have let us go ahead without turning up himself. (We never had any expectations that he would be there.) Or, David could have come for the beginning, and left as soon as the Guest-of-Honour was seated and the screening commenced.

At the UNICEF Singapore office the next morning, we got together and prepared the biggest, nicest UNICEF greeting card we could find. This is what we wrote inside:

Dear Mrs Glass,

We have not yet met you, but we wanted to tell you that we were moved beyond words when we found out last night, only because we decided on the spur of the moment to invite David to join us for a post-screening dinner, that it was your birthday and that you'd pushed back your celebration for our event. Please accept our warmest and most heartfelt thanks and belated Happy Birthday wishes. We consider it our highest honour to know David, and, through David, you.

With gratitude and thanksgiving,

(all our signatures)

What happened after that?

I did get to meet Wendy (Mrs Glass) and we became very, very special friends. David, Wendy and I became such good friends that he eventually nominated me to run Golden Village after his relocation back to Melbourne to look after his mother. It was my dream job, a perfect confluence of passion and profession! I handed the reins back to David when he and Wendy returned to live in Singapore. Wendy accompanied me to select an engagement ring for Linda, now my lovely wife. Wendy also kept the ring for me, and brought it to the proposal location on that (other) big night, so that I would have one less logistical item to worry about in orchestrating the surprise and popping the Question.

Linda accepted.

And then....

Déjà vu for me.

Planning began. Planning for a different kind of event, but at a rather familiar venue.

The UNICEF movie venue.

My *alma mater*.

My emotional home.

We held our wedding at Golden Village — the first-ever processional and solemnisation service in a Singapore cinema hall. David and Wendy were our hosts and witnesses.

Dreams do come true.

Even if (in fact, especially if) one does not plan that way at the outset.

My hobby helped a good cause, and ended up becoming my job.

My playground was my workplace… and where my dream girl became my wife.

Thanks to *Miracle on 34th Street*.

Thanks to UNICEF.

A Christmas to Remember

Carolyn Tay

From her involvement as a team member of the then largest corporate donor to UNICEF Singapore in 1992, Carolyn Tay became a regular volunteer. She recounts how she came to make a personal commitment to UNICEF and how the experience helped to affirm her belief in the generosity of Singaporeans.

The brief for Christmas that year was "to do something different and meaningful, and to give back to the community". Thanks to the management team of the then Hyatt Regency Singapore hotel (Hyatt), I began my relationship with UNICEF Singapore in 1992.

It was the usual practice of most hotels during that time to spend quite a generous amount of money on the Christmas and New Year festivities. This included designing and printing Christmas cards to send yuletide greetings to their customers and business associates as well as decorating various public areas in the hotel to create a festive atmosphere for the Christmas season. It was no different at the Hyatt when I was working with them. Christmas and New Year were major celebrations and we usually tried our best to outdo ourselves each year especially with regard to Christmas decorations.

However, in 1992, the management team decided to dispense with the usual routine of sending Christmas cards and decking out the hotel, except for one big tree in the hotel lobby. The savings would go towards a good cause. It was a novel and bold move at that time. There were several discussions on which causes to support and how to go about it. Eventually, the hotel decided to organise a lunch at a children's home and a tea at The Missionaries of Charity for their residents, hosted by the hotel's management team and staff. The balance of the savings would be donated to a beneficiary that reflected Hyatt International's global presence. After much research, UNICEF was the unanimous choice.

UNICEF believes that "all children have a right to survive, thrive and fulfil their potential — to the benefit of a better world." It is their mission to fight for this right on behalf of children all around the world, regardless of nationality, in developed and developing countries. UNICEF's extensive range of programmes, in all corners of the world, looks at children's rights, survival, development and protection. This mission resonated deeply with each member of the Hyatt's management team. Long before corporate social responsibility became a buzzword, Hyatt International Hotels were all acutely aware of their responsibility as corporate citizens. As an organisation with a global reach, UNICEF still succeeded in establishing deep ties with each community that it operated in. This reflected Hyatt International's strategy of a global reach with a strong local presence.

And so this was my introduction to UNICEF Singapore. Hyatt donated S\$20,000[1] to UNICEF's programme in Somalia, which was suffering from a terrible drought that year. And although I left Hyatt shortly afterwards, my relationship with UNICEF continued.

In the course of my research, I met Penny Whitworth, Manager of UNICEF Singapore and Peggy Kek, who led the volunteer programme, amongst many other activities she spearheaded at UNICEF. Soon after, Peggy persuaded me to sign up as a volunteer. The UNICEF Singapore volunteers will attest to the fact that it is very hard to say "no" to Peggy. As a volunteer, I assisted mainly with the fundraising activities, and some general administrative duties.

One of the main fundraising programmes I was involved in was the sale of UNICEF merchandise through pop-up sales stands wherever and whenever we could secure the opportunity, especially during the year-end festive season. Shopping centres, corporate events, retail outlets — we welcomed every invitation. One such opportunity was at the Sundowners' gatherings which we were very kindly invited to by the organisers quite regularly. Most of these Sundowners' events were held in watering holes which were rather dimly lit and quite rowdy — not the most conducive environment for selling merchandise, regardless of how deserving the cause. Notwithstanding all the challenges (bearing in mind that these were networking events for young executives who had objectives quite different to ours), we managed to achieve rather good sales. I spent many happy hours pouncing on and cornering these executives who were there for their Happy Hour.

---

[1] Editors' note: Until then, this was the biggest donation that a commercial entity in Singapore had made to UNICEF Singapore.

Despite the setting, these executives were more often than not, well-meaning and quite sympathetic to the cause of improving the lives of children.

Another regular supporter was the now defunct Borders bookstore in the shopping mall, Wheelock Place, where we had one of our busiest sales stands in the few weeks leading up to Christmas. Wheelock Place is situated on Orchard Road, Singapore's main shopping street. I have a soft spot for the mall's security personnel who allowed us to set up our stand in the atrium just in front of the entrance to Borders (even if it might have meant having to bend the rules just a little). This was a prime spot to catch passers-by entering the building compared to the much quieter corner that we were originally assigned. By the time Christmas rolled by, we were quite friendly with the security "uncles" who sometimes even helped us with our heavy boxes of UNICEF merchandise.

The merchandise that we sold at these sales stands included greeting cards, gift tags, calendars, children's jigsaw puzzles, mugs and so on. The most popular item was a pack of 10 greeting cards and envelopes that sold for S$13.

Thirteen dollars. The cost of five life-saving immunisations for a child. It was a simple and effective message that managed to move even the most hard-hearted. And this message has remained with me after all these years.

Another outreach activity I remember helping with was UNICEF Singapore's annual Open House, when we invited the public to visit the office at International Building to learn more about UNICEF and its programmes. Over a weekend, we screened a video at regular intervals, talked earnestly about the various UNICEF programmes, gave away lots of brochures, sold merchandise and tried to recruit volunteers. The UNICEF office was rather compact so it was a real challenge trying to fit in as much as we could into that modest space, from displays of brochures, to exhibition panels, to merchandise displays, to a screening room for the video — all this while still allowing walking room for our visitors.

The video we screened was titled *341*, which was produced for the World Summit on Children in 1990. This Summit marked the adoption of a Declaration and Plan of Action on the Survival, Protection and Development of Children. It was a simple 13-minute video about children's rights and the outcome of the Declaration which was adopted at the Summit. Every child has one chance and one chance only to grow normally in mind and body. Many children around the world do not have this chance because their basic rights have been taken from them as a result of illness, poverty, malnutrition, dehydration, abuse, lack of education and many other reasons that are preventable. The message was a simple one — a child's right to water, food, healthcare, education, protection must be the single highest priority of every government and it cannot be subject to economic or political uncertainties. Regardless of the number of times we volunteers watched the video, it always brought a lump to our throats and made us all the more resolute to do more. Our visitors would be equally touched by the video and after each screening, there would be many asking how they could help to make a difference.

From the wide range of programmes that included getting children off the streets and into schools, or programmes that lowered the mortality rates of infants by providing vaccines, mosquito nets and clean water supplies, or emergency assistance programmes during disasters, there would invariably be one that struck a chord with our visitors. Regardless of whichever programme it was that resonated with each of them, the universal message was one that everyone understood and connected with.

Preceded by hours of preparation that stretched well into the night, each open house was usually the cause of some anxiety as we were never quite sure how many people would actually walk through the doors. Most times though, whatever we lacked in numbers was more than made up for by the generosity of those who did come. Enlightened parents brought their children to see the small exhibition that we had managed to squeeze into the cramped offices of UNICEF. Children would often end up heartily emptying the contents of their piggy banks to benefit a child somewhere. Young and old came; some were enthusiastic in finding out how they could help, others dropped by just to make a donation. While the objective of the Open House was primarily to raise awareness of the work of UNICEF, I remember I was simply overwhelmed by the spontaneous donations of cash and numerous cheques we tallied up by the end of the day. Many of the donors were happy to remain anonymous. It was times like these that confirmed my belief that Singaporeans are generally a kind-hearted and generous lot.

Besides the festive season which was our busiest period, we were kept gainfully occupied the rest of the year with many hours spent sorting and packing cards, stacking brochures, counting merchandise, stuffing envelopes, among many other administrative duties. Humdrum work that was made less tedious by the company of other volunteers who were committed to and passionate about the UNICEF cause. The volunteers comprised people from all walks of life — students, working professionals, housewives, retirees, and in addition to Singaporeans, I remember constantly meeting people of various nationalities. Besides English, one would often hear many other languages being spoken at UNICEF events — Chinese, French, Italian, Spanish, just to name a few. At the volunteer gatherings hosted by Penny at her home, we would often have potluck with each person contributing a dish and the resulting spread would usually be more impressive than most international buffets found in hotels. It was really wonderful to see people of different nationalities and backgrounds all coming together, focusing on one common goal.

Every child has a right to have access to nutrition, clean water, healthcare, education, a right to be safe and protected, free from harm and abuse, so that he or she can grow and flourish to become the best that they can be. That belief was what brought all these volunteers together in support of UNICEF in its mission to help children all around the world.

I have very fond memories of my volunteer experience with UNICEF Singapore and to this day, I feel honoured that I was able to help in some small way.

Inspired by UNICEF

Simon Fenley

Simon Fenley, a British businessman based in Asia, had his first personal encounter with UNICEF in 1990. Like many others, this was perhaps a "gateway" encounter that convinced him that giving back to the development cause also made good business sense.

My first main interaction with UNICEF was in 1990 when I was living in Thailand. I had to visit Jomtien, Pattaya for a few days and this happened to coincide with the launch of the "Education for All" movement at the World Conference on Education for All by UNESCO, UNDP, UNICEF and the World Bank.

Somehow I managed to get hold of the organisers and persuaded them to let me join the conference. It was a very impressive event with great plans and strategies to change the world. There were many inspiring speeches including ones by the then Director General of UNESCO, Federico Mayor. Participants endorsed an "expanded vision of learning" and pledged to universalise primary education and massively reduce illiteracy by the end of the decade. The event has become a regular global commitment to provide quality basic education for all children, youth and adults.

Fast forward a few years and after living in Hong Kong for a year we arrived in Singapore in 1991. Shortly after arriving my wife and I separated. I now found myself with two beautiful young daughters to take care of, and looking for potential business opportunities. As I had been vegetarian for many years, I decided that my first venture would be a health food restaurant called The Good Life Restaurant, named after Singaporean writer Richard Seah's excellent *The Good Life* publication about natural ways of living better. The restaurant was located in the heart of

Singapore's business district at Boat Quay, on the bank of the Singapore River, and opened in 1993 serving mainly macrobiotic and vegetarian food.

We were new to this business and after rather a long while of getting all the necessary permits, putting in grease traps and other requirements, we were ready to decorate our restaurant. The image we were going for was a rustic one and we were thinking of what types of pictures we should hang on the walls.

We found some old pictures of Boat Quay, which we had originally thought were 100 to 200 years old, but were actually only 30 to 40 years old; it was amazing to discover how fast Singapore had been developing over a very short time. In the end we decided to combine our desire for the rustic with our love of developmental work. We also hoped to purchase in a way that would also prove of benefit to others. So we approached UNICEF to see if they had any photos they could allow us to use to decorate the restaurant in exchange for a donation to their activities.

We found some very beautiful rural pictures of houses in Cambodia and other developing countries which we hung in the main area of the restaurant. In other areas we hung some of UNICEF's more provocative posters, like the one my elder daughter still remembers to this day, which had a picture of a young boy. The words on the poster were "What do you want to be when you grow up?" Then at the bottom of the poster it had the word in big bold letters "Alive". We also hoped that by displaying UNICEF's photos, it would also in some way help to spread awareness of the great work it does.

Oh, in case you're wondering how our health food restaurant fared on Boat Quay, we did very well at lunchtime and grew to have quite a following. However, the evening crowd did not really justify the investment we had made in the business. It seemed particularly around the Boat Quay area that after work people were more interested in having a few fun drinks to relax and the more health-conscious crowd would head home.

By then, we had opened a health food store in Orchard Point and had started to develop our natural products wholesale business, Essential Living, which we still operate today, that distributes natural health, wellness and beauty products in Singapore, Malaysia and the Philippines. So in 1993, we sold our restaurant and if I recall correctly, it was quickly turned into a seafood restaurant selling mostly oysters.

Of course back when sending physical Christmas cards was the thing to do, we used to enjoy visiting the UNICEF offices and buying our cards from them and for a while even sold some from our store in Orchard Point.

Another of our projects that has been on the back burner for many years is World Monitor. This has also been greatly inspired by the works of the United Nations and its sister organisations like UNICEF. I remember in 1983, I was backpacking through India and coming into Calcutta from the west on the train. We started to travel through the Calcutta slums and I was shocked to find that even after an hour on the train we were still travelling through the same slums.

Having had such experiences and knowing of the wonderful work that UNICEF and so many amazing NGOs do around the world has greatly inspired us to develop projects under World Monitor. Soon we will be launching our wiki for charities at WikiCharity.org and our worldwide educational portal at WorldMonitorRoom.com.

Another experience that has greatly influenced me was when I saw a beautiful video of an eye camp put together by the charitable organisation Prasad. They had set up a temporary hospital in some of the poorest parts of India. Doctors, surgeons, nurses all volunteered their time and they performed hundreds of cataract surgeries for free over a few days.

It was amazing to see the delight on the faces of people who could now see again. However, it was also obvious that those that who volunteered also derived great benefit from creating such happiness in other people's lives, possibly even more than those they helped. So an idea came to me one day, that perhaps those who live in poverty and hunger are actually great souls who have been willing to take on these roles to give us in the more developed parts of our planet the opportunity and benefit of being able to assist them. Though if you do decide you wish to become involved in such a great movement, then how do you know how best to assist? How do you know that the funds or time you donate are not just being used in a wasteful fashion? Well this is where we would like World Monitor to help make such a difference. Although this organisation has many other aspects to it, our main goal has gradually developed to be: To support others to make a difference.

I feel that corporations can be one of the most powerful ways to improve our world. In our own small way, we try to ensure that the work we do has more at its core than just making money and we look to ensure that we share by donating profits from our businesses to other worthy causes. For instance, with the assistance of one of my daughters, we have recently launched a new beauty site, Phi-Localy.com, which also donates a proportion of the profit from the sale of each product to organisations that work to make our world a more beautiful place.

Another project we are involved in is waternexus.org, which looks for opportunities to support communities in need to obtain clean water, which should really be a basic human right. Our work is currently focused in the Philippines, but we hope eventually to have created successful models that can be expanded into many other countries.

Whilst it would seem to be a good practice for all of us to have a more altruistic attitude, I also feel quite strongly that this also makes good business sense. It seems that consumers are more willing to purchase products from companies that act in such ways that benefit a greater good than just themselves. It does not have to cost the consumers more. If companies are willing to give away part of the profits they make, I believe the increase in sales volumes they achieve will more than counteract any loss in margin. So everyone wins. Consumers feel happier about their purchases, companies make more money, and charities and NGOs receive more donations.

Our hope is that from being inspired by the work of such great organisations preceding us that we can be guided by what has proved successful and do whatever we can in our small way to contribute to making this world a better place in which we and our future generations can live.

The Art of Giving

Penny Whitworth

Penny Whitworth worked for UNICEF for over 30 years in Geneva, Singapore and New York. She worked in the UNICEF Singapore office as Greeting Card Operation Manager from 1991 to 1994 and Market Development Officer Asia from 1994 to 1998. In this essay she describes the evolution of the sales of UNICEF greeting cards, the role the Singapore office played and how artists from the city-state contributed to UNICEF efforts to promote child survival, development, protection and participation.

From its inception, UNICEF has been a lean organisation with limited resources to deliver programmes for the well-being of all children everywhere. UNICEF is funded entirely by voluntary contributions from governments and individuals. This was the reason why a number of fundraising ideas were developed from the very beginning of the organisation's existence. The UNICEF greeting card is one of the key activities that helped to turn UNICEF into a household name. Some of the organisation's most precious collaborators are those who offer their services, time and talents free of charge. They include artists and volunteers whose efforts come together in the sale of UNICEF cards and gifts. The UNICEF greeting card programme has come to embody this unique type of support. It was launched in 1949. Sixty-six years of worldwide fundraising activity for UNICEF has generated over US\$4.2 billion through the sale of more than 5 billion cards in over 100 countries. According to the UNICEF annual report for 2015, revenue from the sale of cards and gifts in 2014 totalled US\$43 million.

The story of how the greeting cards began is part of UNICEF folklore. The first design was a picture of a maypole painted on glass by a seven-year-old Czechoslovakian girl. Dzitka and her classmates were regular drinkers of UNICEF milk, and the paintings they produced were a "thank-you", sent off to UNICEF's bureau in Prague by their teacher. From there, the glass picture of children dancing round the maypole went to Vienna, where staff member, Grace Holmes Barbey, sent out on an information gathering mission, wrapped it up and took it back to New York. In October 1949, small numbers of a card using Dzitka's design were produced as a modest fundraiser.

From *The Children and the Nations* by Maggie Black (1986, p. 68)

From those small beginnings, little could that schoolteacher imagine the impact of her initiative to send off those thank-you paintings.

At that time, few realised the potential these cards represented to educate the world on the pressing needs of children and as a source of funds to meet those needs. Into the concept of traditional greeting cards, UNICEF introduced the new idea of using designs of world-famous artists including contemporaries such as Dufy, Chagall, Miro and Picasso. The collections also introduced indigenous art forms from around the world; one of the earliest sets was created by the Cape Dorset artists Ikaluk, Kananginak, Mungituk, Niviaksiak and Pootagook on Baffin Island. These artists, like so many others, waived the reproduction rights for UNICEF to print their works as cards.

Care was taken at first to avoid linking the cards, in words or pictures, to Christmas or any faith-based celebration. The greeting was printed in the official languages of the United Nations. Individuals and companies could count on the high standards of reproduction and printing of UNICEF cards to match the unique art they reproduced and the universal commitment to making the world a better place for children. In time designs were introduced to celebrate seasonal and sacred occasions.

There are several stages before a card reaches the sales venues, catalogues or today, e-shops. The initial selection is done by art specialists who research and collect designs that correspond to themes and styles that today mark a number of cultural and religious celebrations such as Christmas, New Year, Eid and birthdays, in addition to images that are suited for note cards for general occasions. The designs are sourced directly from artists, illustrators and museums. These visuals are presented at a meeting each year to representatives of the countries where they are to be sold, to choose cards that are suitable for individuals or companies. The choices are based on market research and trends and sales statistics. One such meeting was held for the region in Singapore in 1990. Later these meetings came to take place at a central location to pick the cards for the global, regional and local collections.

Lunar New Year cards were printed in Singapore in 1988 for the first time, for sale in 1989. The cards included scenes from the Autumn Mountains in China, paintings of Chinese carp by Malaysian artist Chuah Seow Keng, and gold-embossed Chinese characters, paintings of a dragon and phoenix, and gold-embossed flowers. Hari Raya cards were printed in 1989 for the first time in Singapore, for sale in 1990. They were sold in Singapore and distributed throughout the region. Those first cards featured calligraphic verses by Jordanian artists, decoupage prints and paintings from Turkey, Morocco, Syria, Iran and Kuwait.

Over the years a number of artists from Singapore have given generously of their works to UNICEF for cards to be sent on a variety of occasions. They include *Lantern* and *Floating Village* by Tay Bak Koi; *Good Wishes* and *Good Fortune* by Yong Cheong Thye; *Joyful Abundance* by Cristene Chang Hoei; *Dog of Prosperity* by Berwin See; and a stationery set featuring *Glowing* by Lee Hock Moh. *Mother and Daughter* by Cheong Soo Pieng was also reproduced on stationery sets. All of these designs perfectly met one of the most important criteria for UNICEF, a design particular to the culture of the artist that at the same time held universal meaning and appeal.

It was the typically Singaporean nature of Tay's works and the themes they express that had appeal for UNICEF. At that time, the expert who led the team that sourced designs from around the world was in Singapore. She said of the first card that the design, colouring and the serene harbourscape, reminiscent of a bygone era depicting sampans and junks, represented "a mood and harmonious feeling" particular to Singaporean art, a style that was not seen elsewhere. Added to the harmony and peace of this watercolour with the inimitable brush strokes of the artist is the visual reminder of the individual making her or his way through life. His approach that mixed realism and fantasy, often in an urban landscape, appealed widely to UNICEF customers. With great humility, the artist was surprised and pleased that his works were selected for UNICEF cards. At the time he said, "When I do good things, I feel happy. I have no other way of helping these children except through art."

When I had the privilege to visit Tay to thank him for his contributions and, on behalf of the team in New York, to see if he had another painting he would like to contribute, I too was struck by the quiet vigour of this down-to-earth, generous and gracious artist. In his home, surrounded by his latest paintings, we communicated more through our eyes and gestures than words as he did not speak much English, and I even less Chinese. I was able to feel and see the great passion, joy and love he held for each of his works, as he presented them, though he was fonder of one or two. On another occasion I visited Mr Tay with the intent of acquiring one of his pieces. While I was inclined towards one or two works, he quietly steered me in the direction of a relatively abstract landscape wrought from dark earthy hues, with hints of his distinctive pinks and gold with the signature nod to humanity in the form of a few people. I followed his lead without really knowing why. The work still has a prominent position in my home, and I continue to wonder why he believed this was the piece for me.

Since the principal goal of my work with UNICEF was to promote awareness and help to generate funds, I generally had little direct contact with contributing artists. On the few occasions that I was asked to represent the art-sourcing team in Singapore or elsewhere, it was always a treat to exchange a few words and to follow these creative beings in their own setting, sometimes a studio, sometimes a kitchen, sometimes at an exhibition. So it was with Yong Cheong Thye, a master Chinese calligrapher who donated a number of designs to UNICEF. His works were perfect for the Lunar New Year line with bold brush strokes and a contemporary approach combined with the traditional. I visited Master Yong several times at his gallery. In the midst of the bustle of the city, a sense of stillness and tranquillity radiated out to greet the visitor. It was not an inactive calm as it also served as a workshop and studio. In addition to the designs for UNICEF, I had the joy and honour to work with Master Yong on a calligraphy for my own collection; it is a treasure.

The contribution of these artists was celebrated in an exhibition at the Hyatt Regency Hotel in January 1994, called "Artists for the Children of the World". Developed to celebrate 40 years of UNICEF greeting cards, 30 panels that travelled the world illustrating many of the artworks used for UNICEF cards, were on view. Some revealed the works of the most illustrious artists, others the variety of themes like family, peace and ecology, and a diversity of motifs such as children, flowers, landscapes, calligraphy, seasonal symbols, globes and doves that were used over the years. Four of the artists from Singapore were present at the opening together with originals of some of their works. It was thrilling to have the artists present mingling with the viewers, UNICEF volunteers and staff. Lee Hock Moh attended with his painting, *Glowing*. The standard UNICEF cards are approximately the same size as a printed photo (11 × 15.5cm), whereas Mr Lee had to stretch his arms apart to hold the original painting, a marvellous cascade of orchids seeming to burst from a grove of bamboo towards a quiet stretch of water watched over by a pair of birds.

Artists over the past 70 years have gained a deep satisfaction from sharing their work knowing how their works helped children. Many UNICEF supporters around the world were pleased that their support be carried through exceptional images, some companies were so satisfied that they commissioned UNICEF to request a number of artists for bespoke designs for their seasonal greeting cards. The sense of fulfilment expressed by Tay Bak Koi is one that is echoed by everyone engaged in contributing in their own way to the cause of making the world a safer and happier place for children.

Section 4

Reflections

From Academic to Development Worker

Ng Shui-Meng with Peggy Kek[1]

Dr Ng Shui-Meng is a Singaporean who worked with UNICEF from 1986, retiring in 2008 after her last post as UNICEF Representative in Timor-Leste. In this interview, she reflects on her career choices, the challenges of a development worker, the changes she has observed in how UNICEF operates, what she was able to bring to her postings as a Singaporean, and her advice to younger Singaporeans interested in a career in international development.

Q: *How did you transition from your career in academia to development?*

Ng Shui-Meng (NSM): When I received the scholarship from ISEAS[2] to do my graduate studies at the University of Hawaii's East-West Centre (EWC), the Vietnam War was still ongoing. ISEAS wanted somebody to specialise in the area of Vietnam, Laos and Cambodia. After I finished my PhD in 1979, I came back and worked at ISEAS, first as Fellow, then Senior Fellow.

By then I had met Sombath, my husband, when he was doing a degree in agronomy in Hawaii.[3] He had always wanted to go back to Laos and was going back and forth between Hawaii and Vientiane since 1978. He was trying to find out whether he would have opportunities to work in Laos, get an understanding of the new government and what the areas of need in Laos might be. In 1984, he finally returned to Laos. It would be peace for the first time after many years of conflict, and Laos had a chance to renew itself. I was always idealistic. Since the

[1] This account is based on an interview by Peggy Kek on 6 June 2015.
[2] The Institute of Southeast Asian Studies (ISEAS) is based in Singapore.
[3] While in Hawaii, Shui-Meng met and, eventually in 1983, married Sombath Somphone, a highly respected community development worker from Laos who founded PADETC. Since he went missing in Laos in December 2012, she has been working tirelessly to find him.

focus of my research had been Vietnam, Laos and Cambodia, it would be a good opportunity for me to get to understand these countries, more on the ground than just from an academic perspective. So I kept an open mind and in 1985, I joined Sombath in Vientiane.

My first experience in development was thanks to Quaker Laos, a non-governmental organisation (NGO). I was hired to do a study into gender dynamics in the local communities. But first I had to learn the language.

Lao language is a bit like Malay — no complicated grammar structures, no tenses, and it does not matter if you mix up the order of the words, people can still understand you. It's a tonal language, which wasn't such a barrier with my background in Chinese. When I had picked up enough of the language, we went to the field to learn about their needs, and the gender and household dynamics in the decision-making in the community.

Then in early 1988, when I was in Bangkok, an old professor of mine told me that he had heard that UNICEF Laos was looking for a consultant. He made the introductions and soon after I went back to Vientiane, I got a call from UNICEF Laos.

The assignment was to carry out what would be the first situation analysis of the children in Laos. UNICEF needed the analysis done in order to design the national country programme for Laos. I finished the study and was asked to do another study, this time on the EPI (Expanded Programme for Immunisation). And that was how I started working for UNICEF.

Q: What were your experiences working for UNICEF in Laos and thereafter?

NSM: The UNICEF Laos office was very small then. There was the Representative, the Programme Officer who was also the Health Officer, a Water and Sanitation officer, an Education officer, and a few local staff who were responsible for supplies and support services. At the end of 1988, a vacancy opened up for a programme officer for education. I applied and was accepted, and that's how I became a UNICEF staff member.

The position was responsible for both education and women's development. Both programmes were community-based and allowed me to travel all over Laos. From 1989 to 1996, I did a lot of fieldwork, which really helped me to strengthen my knowledge of this country with small, ethnically and culturally diverse communities spread out over a large land area.[4]

---

[4] See Ng Shui-Meng's "Improving Children's Lives in Laos" in this volume.

I left for China in 1996 for a position in the area of Social Development Programme for Poor Areas (SPPA), which also ran a community level project targeting women. At that time, in the mid-1990s, the concept of microfinance was just emerging. The programme objective was to make an impact on the well-being of children by building women's capacity through the use of micro-credit.[5]

Then in 2000, I came back to UNICEF Laos as the Deputy Representative and Senior Programme Officer. I wasn't responsible for a sectoral programme but each sector had to be part of the big framework and I spent more time in meetings coordinating the Country Programme.

After that, in 2004, I went to Timor-Leste. I thought Timor-Leste, being a newly independent country, would be quite an interesting posting and it would be my last posting before retirement.[6]

I knew it would be a challenge. And it *was* very challenging. It reminded me of when I first came to Laos: a country in post-war reconstruction, with a great deal of political re-adjustment going on. In a post-war society, the needs are everywhere so it's important to focus on the priority areas. In countries with many needs, where it's not very developed, government agencies typically also develop a trust for UNICEF, at least in countries that I've worked in. We were able to respond in very concrete ways to the needs of the country, where you can see the results readily and they will have impact on the people, especially the children.

Q: How has UNICEF changed over the time that you were with the organisation?

NSM: UNICEF staff used to go to the field a lot. By the time I retired in 2008, I found that staff had less and less time touching the ground.

We spent a lot more time in meetings, in planning and in making sure that our resources were not misused or misdirected. There are now computerised programmes for everything for spending money and reporting. This is all done in the name of management excellence and transparency. In principle, it's good. There should be reporting and coordination, in a major company or organisation.

But the reporting requirements consume a lot of the time of UNICEF staff and we can end up relying only on the local staff or the local government partners to report back on what's being done in the field. Of course, the government partners are the ones implementing the programmes and they should be mainly the ones doing the work in the field. But as UNICEF staff, we should still have a good feel of what's happening on the ground, to make sure that we are swift-footed enough

---

[5] See Ng Shui-Meng's "The Power of a Little Trust and Credit" in this volume.
[6] See Ng Shui-Meng's "Emergency Mode in Timor-Leste" in this volume.

to change or adapt. The Country Programme Framework is there as a guide, but it should never be written in stone. Many of the development agencies are now being consumed by making and following log frames, and reporting on the basis of what we put into the log frames. We have lost a little bit of that flexibility and human touch. We've become more bureaucratic.

At a macro level, we may be able to show that globally, as well as regionally, we have been able to contribute more to policy development, supporting the governments to meet their MDGs.[7] But I think we have lost touch with some of the reality.

UNICEF has always been an organisation where the field office had, not a lot, but enough, autonomy. Now it's become less flexible for the field, to be in line with what Headquarters (HQ) decides, with HQ operating more as a "think tank" and the directives filtering down to the field. The individual in the field still has some flexibility if he or she is willing to think outside the box and to base decisions on the reality of the needs in the field; but much less than before.

Q: You mentioned that UNICEF is well trusted. Why do you think that is so?

NSM: I think the way UNICEF works is very practical. The work is contributing directly to the welfare of the target groups of people. So we build trust along the way. Where we are most effective is where we have a good relationship with the local government, and local community leadership, and not only with the central government. And that kind of relationship stems from both the work in the capital, and also in the field. But it also depends a lot on the kind of people that UNICEF chooses to hire.

Q: What sort of qualities do you find in people who work for UNICEF?

NSM: The work UNICEF does makes people feel they are doing something really meaningful and useful. Most people that I know and have worked with in UNICEF feel it's not just a job.

UNICEF is able to motivate its staff quite well. It could also be the leadership. The Executive Director Jim Grant brought a different kind of leadership that was quite different from Carol Bellamy. You may like them or not for whatever reason, but they are inspirational leaders. Both of them, and also the people around them, the Deputies and so on — they were people at the top who could inspire.

---

[7] Millennium Development Goals.

And what UNICEF always makes the staff feel, is that we are family. Whether you believe it or not, somehow we are there, together.

There are not many jobs where you feel good about what you do every day. There's a sense of purpose and therefore it's easier to bring out commitment from the staff. You may be tired and some of the meetings are boring. But, at the end of the day, you ask why are we here? What are we trying to do? Who are we trying to reach? Who can benefit from what we do?

And somehow you feel that it's actually a privilege to be able to work in an organisation like UNICEF. You feel fulfilled while working with UNICEF. Of course different people have different personalities. But by and large, the kind of people who work at UNICEF feel this way.

Q: *What was it like working in UNICEF as a Singaporean?*

NSM: Until I joined UNICEF in my mid-30s, my world had been fairly Singapore-based and also very academic. Working in a multilateral organisation like UNICEF, I felt that I had gained a lot by looking at the world from a much wider perspective, quite different than thinking from a Singaporean perspective.

There are so many colleagues from different cultures, and each one brings with him or her cultural baggage. I was able to learn new ways of interaction and you have to adjust. It was really a great privilege to be immersed into such a diverse environment. Most rewarding of all was the chance to interact with the local staff of the different countries I have served. They are the ones that can make us understand best the cultures and society that we work in. Listening to their perspectives was, for me, very important and crucial if we wanted our work to be relevant and useful.

I learnt to be as open-minded as possible. You may not agree with your colleagues all the time but at least, you see a new way of thinking and doing, and not just a right or wrong way.

Q: *In terms of building a career in UNICEF — did being a Singaporean make it easier, or harder?*

NSM: In the UN or other agencies in the development world, NGOs, IFIs[8], the Singaporean reputation is one of being hardworking, competent, well educated. I think Singaporeans are regarded, by and large, very well.

---

[8]International financial institutions (such as the World Bank and the International Monetary Fund).

I've been asked many times why there are so few Singaporeans working in multilateral agencies. When I was working in UNICEF, we didn't get many applications from Singaporeans. I think even up till today not many Singaporeans know too much about the different types of work the UN is involved in. They may only know about the work of the UN General Assembly. I think there are many more Singaporeans who can contribute to the work of the various UN Agencies in different parts of the world. It would also benefit many of these agencies to have more Singaporeans working in them.

Q: *What would you say to encourage more Singaporeans to pursue a career in an international development agency like UNICEF? And if they were interested, what should they do to increase their chances of getting a job with any of these UN agencies?*

NSM: I'd say, outside of the nice secure world of Singapore, they would learn about new ways of doing things, about a whole different world out there.

And if they were interested, they should gain some experience. A lot of young Singaporeans are already travelling. But they should go beyond just being a tourist. They should drop their rucksack, get to know the culture, the people, spend a bit of time. Yes, there will be discomfort and they will not have the usual amenities they are used to in Singapore. But, don't worry about the inconvenience. Be willing to take some risks. And if you want a career with a UN agency, you have to have a sense of curiosity and a willingness to learn. That's very important.

Q: *What would you like to see as the next phase of UNICEF-Singapore engagement?*

NSM: Well, for all that I've said about the practical value of UNICEF's fieldwork, UNICEF has also done a lot, globally, to build up a very strong scholarship and understanding about children. Both in terms of rights and in terms of what kind of world there should be for children.

Singapore has always prided itself as a knowledge centre — IT centre, banking centre and so on. It would be an advantage if an organisation like UNICEF were to build up a knowledge centre for children and young people in Singapore and Asia. It would add a much more human face to Singapore, than this hard, efficient, competent face.

Right now, the UNICEF's main knowledge centre is Innocenti[9], which is very European-based. It's a different set of issues that children face in European

---

[9] Innocenti is the Office of Research in Florence, Italy, that UNICEF established in 1988. See http://www.unicef-irc.org.

situations. The Asian context is different. It would be great for UNICEF to have a bigger footprint, to have a knowledge centre for children and young people in Singapore, covering the region. It would be both a good thing for Singapore, and I firmly believe, a good thing also for UNICEF.

From Journalist to HIV-AIDS Adviser

Cheng Wing-Sie with Peggy Kek[1]

Cheng Wing-Sie is a Singaporean who joined UNICEF in 1987 and is currently the Senior Adviser/Regional HIV and AIDS Adviser based in the UNICEF Regional Office for East Asia and the Pacific (EAPRO). As of 2015, she has worked for UNICEF for 27 years and counting. Here she recounts where her career with the organisation has brought her — geographically and in terms of meeting the development demands of the day.

A Phone Call... From UNICEF

I started my career with UNICEF in 1987. I was working for the then Singapore Broadcasting Corporation as a reporter, covering high technology. One day, I received a phone call from the UNICEF office here in Singapore, asking me to meet a visiting Director of Public Information and External Affairs from UNICEF New York, who wanted to interview me for a job in New York. As I hadn't applied for any job and didn't know anything about UNICEF at the time, I was baffled and curious and quickly went to the library to read up about UNICEF before showing up the next day at the UNICEF office.

I met John Williams, a lovely Australian gentleman who told me he was here interviewing seven Asian journalists. He said that UNICEF, being part of the United Nations, was looking for more Asian faces to join their communications team, which was then too Anglicised. This job was to edit copy for all the updates from communications offices around the world, for an in-house newsletter. After hearing him describe the duties and responsibilities, I said, "Thank you, Mr Williams, for considering me but I'm a very young journalist with limited

[1] This account is based on an interview by Peggy Kek on 29 April 2015.

editorial experience. I'm only 25 years old and have been working as a broadcast journalist for only three years. And, English is not my first language." He asked me more about my first language, Chinese, and asked me to bring him my CV the next day.

Ten months later, when I had forgotten about this encounter (daily news reporting did keep one very busy) I received a long-distance call from UNICEF China, from a Dr Manzoor Ahmed, who turned out to be the UNICEF Representative for China and was also a renowned educationist from Bangladesh. Dr Manzoor asked if I would consider a posting to Beijing. They were setting up an information unit and needed someone who could communicate effectively — read, write and speak — in Chinese as well as English. He flew over two weeks later to interview me in Singapore and that's how I ended up in UNICEF.

UNICEF in China, Post-Cultural Revolution

I was in Beijing from 1987 to 1992. It was a challenging time to be in China. The country had barely emerged from a decade of chaos from the Cultural Revolution and was just starting to adopt an "open-door" policy. Fear and apprehension were still very much everywhere. New ideas were cautiously received, if not rejected.

My job was to set up an information office to advocate for UNICEF and the UN's global agenda for children. Foremost, the goals were to immunise all children to spare them unnecessary death and ill health from childhood tuberculosis, measles, whooping cough, diphtheria and polio — all common killers and cripplers of infants that are preventable by vaccines. Second, we needed to prevent infant and child death from diarrheal dehydration by educating parents and caregivers on the use of oral rehydration salts (ORS). Third was to protect pregnant mothers from malnutrition such as iron and Vitamin A deficiency disorders that could severely affect birth, and to improve antenatal care for mothers. Finally, we had to make sure that all the children went to school and completed at least primary education.

As a UN entity, UNICEF's role was not to deliver these services but to work with governments to make sure these services reached all children and families, especially those in rural and remote areas. We brought in technical expertise and financial assistance requested by the government. UNICEF's catalytic funding of US$10 million in immunisation at that time, for instance, had elicited a US$100 million investment from the Chinese government to improve routine immunisation for all children.

My role was to organise advocacy meetings with central and local governments. I also had to prepare Chinese materials, organise translation, edit, publicise them in the official daily press, as well as distribute them to different government partners.

My job also carried a fundraising responsibility. I had to accompany many donors to various project sites, which gave me the opportunity to travel to many remote areas of China to witness UNICEF's programmes for mothers and children that were implemented in partnership with local authorities. These visits took me to Xinjiang (at the border with Pakistan), Sichuan, Shanxi, Shandong, Guizhou, Yunnan, Guangxi and other provinces, where programmes on immunisation and maternal care were being scaled up or piloted.

I was also assigned the additional responsibility of promoting the sale of UNICEF greeting cards, on a small scale, in China. This aspect of the job took me to the more industrialised cities of Shanghai, Guangzhou, Shenzhen and Tianjin where I persuaded, quite successfully, major hotels to sell the cards in their hotel shops. Many of these hotels and other multinational companies also bought these cards in bulk to send Christmas, year-end and Chinese New Year greetings to their clients. Subsequently, when the sales operation had grown too big, the Country Representative decided to hire someone to take charge of it full-time.

In Bangkok: Mobilising for the Convention on the Rights of the Child

Next, I moved to Bangkok as a social mobilisation and external affairs officer. The job title was different, but I was still supporting public communications. More specifically, I was brought in to support the work to mobilise governments in East Asia-Pacific to ratify the Convention on the Rights of the Child (CRC), which guarantees the rights of every child to healthcare, education, protection, information and development.

I helped to organise numerous CRC consultations in different countries, including visits of CRC Committee members to dialogue with political leaders in the region. In the process, I had a chance to meet several dignitaries, including Bishop Desmond Tutu of South Africa, Professor Vitit Muntarbhorn of Thailand, and many of the outstanding international human rights advocates from Brazil, Barbados, Portugal, Philippines, Burkina Faso, Russia and Sweden. I also organised press conferences for them. It was a lot of fun and I learned a great deal about international covenants and how they worked. I ended up spending four wonderful years in Thailand from 1992 to 1996.

Organising the Asia Media Summit for Child Rights and Heading to Harvard

Since my days in China, I had also started to take a huge interest in Communication for Development, or C4D for short. It was a different type of communication, more like social marketing with specific "behavioural change" targets. In addition to writing press releases, organising press conferences and advocacy meetings, I wanted to learn more about the work that went into changing public behaviour, measuring change in behaviours and attitudes, translating information into knowledge, through social ads, edutainment and designing survey research to measure how new behaviours were adopted as a result.

I also felt that I needed to recharge my mind. I decided to do a Master's degree, to learn statistics and social marketing techniques that were fundamental to C4D. I decided to give Harvard a try. The application process was tough, entailing tests, papers and an interview. That year, 1996, I was also in the middle of organising an Asia Media Summit for Child Rights, in partnership with an influential organisation — the Asia Broadcasting Union (ABU) — as well as the Australian and Philippine Children's TV Foundations. The event was aimed at rallying the media to support child rights and improving media practices in respect of children. I had come up with the idea of the Summit because at that time I was hanging out with a great friend from ABU as well as the TV Foundations. Together, we just decided to do it. My boss had left for a big job in the UN Human Rights Commission then. I was pretty much operating alone together with the partners, while shouldering the rigorous requirements for admission to Harvard.

We pulled off the Summit in July 1996 in Manila — there were 500 attendees from all over Asia — officiated by then President Fidel V Ramos. It was a huge event and the first of its kind in Asia. The Summit had left its mark, judging from the subsequent increased media engagements in child rights issues. The UNICEF Deputy Executive Director, Stephen Lewis, also came to the Summit. He was curious about how I had managed to rally media executives and political leaders from around Asia to support the Summit — being a young, junior officer — and asked about my career plan. I told him that I was planning to go to Harvard and he agreed to help with a training grant to cover half of the tuition fees. Two months later, I enrolled in Harvard as an Edward S Mason Fellow at the Kennedy School.

Defending UNICEF in New York

When I finished my Masters, I was asked by UNICEF to go to New York to cover for a colleague who was going on maternity leave. The job was in the media section of its Division of Communication and I was tasked as the media focal point for HIV and AIDS, which was fast becoming a pandemic at that time. For the next several months, I would work under immense pressure as UNICEF's position on exclusive breastfeeding for children born to HIV-positive mothers was publicly condemned.

Little did I know that the assignment would lay the foundation for my future as a UNICEF Adviser for HIV/AIDS.

UNICEF went through a very rough patch. The organisation was under vehement attack by infant formula producers for our stance on exclusive breast-feeding, including for babies born to HIV-positive mothers. This was 1998 and HIV was an emerging issue.

Even though there is a 33% chance of passing on the virus from mother to child, UNICEF had insisted that exclusive breastfeeding should continue for the first six months. The benefits of breastmilk — at least for the two-thirds who would not be infected and for all other newborns — far outweighed the risk of diarrheal-related death from milk powder mixed with unclean drinking water.

Most mothers in developing countries did not understand those risks associated with using milk powder. Many were also reluctant to switch to bottle-feeding because the majority of mothers in developing countries would breastfeed. Those singled out for formula feeding were easily suspected to be HIV-positive and there was widespread stigma attached to AIDS. The worst was the dual risk of HIV and unclean drinking water from mixed feeding practices. It could easily kill the child.

UNICEF had to deal with a spate of news articles and editorials from many quarters including people whom we suspected had been paid off by commercial infant formula producers to criticise this policy. Of course the UNICEF position that a mother's breastmilk was best for the child went against commercial interest. It threatened their companies' market expansion from urban to rural and remote areas. And there were mothers and babies everywhere so this was a huge multi-million dollar market.

It was an issue fraught with emotions and complexity. Among the host of tasks assigned to me at the time was one that required me to prepare a question-and-answer sheet that UNICEF programme staff in HQ and the field could use to explain our position to the media.

Today, UNICEF has maintained its stance; it is still promoting exclusive breastfeeding everywhere in the world.

Deepening the Work on HIV-AIDS Issues

After the assignment, I was approached with an opportunity to work on a special assignment with UNAIDS in Bangkok. By December 1998, I was back in Bangkok, working with UNAIDS' Southeast Asia Country Support Team to set up the Asia-Pacific Prevention on Mother-to-Child HIV Transmission (PMTCT) Task Force, and a HIV public education campaign.

I enjoyed this assignment very much, partly because I loved being back in Bangkok, and had a ball of a time organising a public communications campaign. A major opportunity arose at that time to educate the public about safe sex — to help control the surging HIV/AIDS epidemic in Asia and around the world. It was the 13th Asian Games hosted by Thailand in Bangkok. I was able to persuade the organising committee to donate free space to advertise "Play Safe!", a campaign featuring Brazilian footballer Ronaldo as the message Ambassador. Within six weeks, we had the banners out all over the stadia and entrance/exit gates set up for the Asian Games around Thailand!

The mission was completed, and I moved again.

Five Years in Nepal

In June 1999, I moved to Kathmandu, Nepal and stayed there until October 2004. Nepal is a country that held a special charm for me. I loved it. I pulled off some major initiatives there. Foremost was "Chatting with My Best Friend" [2], a long-running radio programme which is still on air today. That's when I really got to use what I learnt — statistics, survey research, translating science creatively into edutainment, and communication for behavioural change.

If there's something I learnt after that year, it's that you really have to systematically crunch numbers. That really helped me. Because you have to do surveys, you have to measure change, monitor change and use the data to create something meaningful as well as plan ahead.

Back to Bangkok

In October 2004, I moved back to Thailand, to EAPRO, the UNICEF Regional Office for East Asia and the Pacific in Bangkok, where I assumed a different role.

Nearly all of the changes in my career emanated from a call, an email and a conversation with some colleagues. I hadn't thought of returning to EAPRO.

---

[2] Please see "Chatting with My Best Friend" in this volume for more details.

While completing my fifth working paper on communication for development — after moving from UNICEF Nepal to the UNICEF Regional Office for South Asia across town in Kathmandu in 2003 — I received a phone call from EAPRO. I was asked if I would be interested in applying for the Regional Adviser position on HIV and AIDS. Having spent almost six years in Nepal on two different assignments, I was ready to move. So I did, back to my favourite city, Bangkok.

The work in a regional office was quite different from that of a country office. As a Regional Adviser for HIV/AIDS, I needed to track the epidemic, understand how it affected children and women, and monitor whether UNICEF's response on the ground was making the difference. AIDS is a complex issue. It also attracted considerable bilateral and private resources. It had claimed many lives at their prime; and become the pandemic of the century. For three years I set up a data hub, building a huge database that collated HIV/AIDS numbers from 25 countries in the Asia-Pacific region.

The idea of making HIV data available online, to everyone and in every way, was quite a breakthrough in 2005 — when governments were still apprehensive about AIDS and many were reluctant to release data to the public. AIDS was, for instance, officially called a "social evil" in one of the countries in Southeast Asia. My interest was to get a clear sense of how HIV was spreading among teenagers and young people in Asia — when sexual activities began — and among pregnant women, who in turn can infect their foetuses. The data hub was a repository of all information for anyone who was working on HIV/AIDS issues. I created it jointly with an epidemiologist from UNAIDS in Bangkok. The idea attracted the interest of the Asian Development Bank (ADB), which invested nearly US$1.6 million to help set it up. It also became UNICEF's first regional collaboration with ADB that subsequently drew the two organisations together — and culminated in a global Memorandum of Understanding.

It has been 11 years. I am still in Bangkok and still working for UNICEF.

For Young Singaporeans Seeking a Career with UNICEF or Any Other UN Agency

I have left home for 27 years. Over time, I have seen a change in young Singaporeans. They are becoming more interested in international affairs and social causes. I do receive many requests for voluntary work with communities to make things better for children of the developing world, children and families in poverty. There are so many bright Singaporeans who can use their skills to solve the world's problems. I think Singaporeans are ready to play a bigger part in global development, in humanitarian responses. And a good way to do so is to join UNICEF. Already, we're so under-represented in the UN and in UNICEF.

Within the UN system, UNICEF is "a fund and a programme". Like UNDP, UNFPA and the WFP, UNICEF is an "implementing" agency, which means the resources it mobilises are used to conduct pilots, improve services, initiate trail-blazing actions, including policy analyses to guide policymaking in countries.

An experience with UNICEF will enable Singaporeans to learn how global goals are translated into policies, programmes and services in countries, and further to communities. There is nothing romantic about development; it is a tough business that requires patience, a problem-solving spirit and openness to differences. You also encounter numerous barriers along the road to change. This will be a great, enormous learning opportunity beyond our very comfortable life in Singapore.

UNICEF does advertise many jobs on its website. Singaporeans should definitely give it a try.

For the Children I Came to Know

Peggy Kek

Peggy Kek is a Singaporean who worked with UNICEF as Assistant Fundraising Officer and consultant from 1991 to 1995, in Singapore, Vietnam and China. Starting in 2002, she was consultant to UNICEF again on several occasions, most recently in 2012. Her relationship with UNICEF has continued over the years as consultant, advisor and volunteer. Here she reflects on the continual efforts of UNICEF — its staff, volunteers and ambassadors — to improve the lives of children.

Today, in a world of advanced scientific knowledge and sophisticated political institutions, children continue to be victims of curable diseases and avoidable wars and other conflicts.

In the early 1990s, when I was working with UNICEF Singapore, a devastating famine in Somalia took more than 300,000 lives and brought to our television sets pictures of severely malnourished children with finger-thin arms and bloated stomachs. UNICEF was in constant fundraising mode to send food, water and medical supplies to save the children from hunger, disease and death.

The 1990s was also the period of the violent civil wars that led to the break-up of Yugoslavia. The bombing in cities like Sarajevo and Dubrovnik would leave a generation of emotionally-scarred children. UNICEF introduced theatre and art therapy to help these children. At the start of the therapy, the children began with very dark drawings of bombed out buildings and injured bodies, often using primarily brown and black colours, with the occasional use of red for blood. As time went on, many children would regain some of their optimism and brighter colours would start to appear in their expressive drawings. UNICEF compiled several of the drawings into a book — *I Dream of Peace: The Images of War by Children of Yugoslavia* — which became one of its most effective advocacy tools.

When I joined UNICEF Singapore in 1991, the office was part of the UNICEF Greeting Card Operation, or GCO as everyone in UNICEF used to call it. It was a small office of four staff headed by Penny Whitworth, and I was brought in to support card sales in the local market, to help raise funds for UNICEF programmes worldwide. In addition to the starving and malnourished children of famine, in the course of my time at UNICEF, I came to know the girl child, the street child, the child labourer, the child soldier, the war child and other vulnerable children in what UNICEF called "especially difficult circumstances".

The Children I Came to Know

Who were these children? The girl child could be an Indian girl who watched her brother go to school. Born into a society that favoured boys and disdained girls, she would be told that school was not for girls and would be put to work at home or on a farm. Some would be arranged to be married while still in their early teens.

The street child was usually an orphan who, left to fend for himself, might spend his days running up to cars at traffic light junctions to beg. Without proper shelter and a permanent home, he might sleep in a cardboard box by the side of a road in Brazil. Street children were prime targets for drug traffickers who could start them on glue-sniffing and from there, lead them to drugs and addiction. Addicted, they were vulnerable to all kinds of abuse, sometimes even by law enforcers like policemen.

The child labourer had poor parents who either needed her help on the farm, or the income that she brought in by working in a toy or match factory in Thailand. Removing the child from work completely was usually not feasible. One solution was to incorporate an agreed number of hours of school into the factory schedule. Wells and hand pumps reduced the number of hours spent fetching water, freeing up precious time for walking to school instead.

The child soldier could be as young as 10 or 12. The AK-47 is a rifle that could be easily stripped and assembled by a child of 10. In the 1990s, he was usually lured by a warring faction in an African country and seduced by the promise of power and protection. Away from his parents, he learnt to be loyal to a warlord and to fight for a cause he hardly even understood.

Likewise for the war child. While not necessarily an agent in violence, she witnessed the atrocities and sustained injuries, physical and psychological. Returning these children to civilian life was one of the most difficult things that UNICEF faced. Once the children had seen, experienced and committed violence including killing, they were denied the prospect of an "innocent childhood". Sadly the war child has again been in the news as their numbers started rising in recent years.

The Power of Gratitude

Penny had come to the Singapore posting from Geneva, which was an important hub for the GCO because the key markets were all in Europe. This was where UNICEF had first turned its attention in 1946 and where UNICEF was a household name. Children who had benefited from UNICEF grew up to be staunch lifelong supporters.

> *I can testify to what UNICEF means to children, because I was among those who received food and medical relief right after World War II... I have a long-lasting gratitude and trust for what UNICEF does.*
>
> Audrey Hepburn, actress and UNICEF Ambassador

In the late 1940s, UNICEF's mandate extended into Asia, including Singapore. But while some older people on the island remembered receiving milk from UNICEF, overall, the organisation did not enjoy a very high level of name recognition. In Singapore in the 1990s, while the acronym UNICEF still rang a faint bell, most people knew little more about it, apart from the fact that it was a charity for children.

Another thing that stood out in the UNICEF "ecosystem" was the multitude of ways that individuals, companies and organisations could be involved in the UNICEF cause, according to one's own means and talent. Without a budget for advertising, UNICEF had to be very creative in getting its name out. There was no email, no Facebook nor LinkedIn then, but we used a range of non-digital social networks. The expatriate community was a huge resource as the brand recognition and support was very high from many of these nationals who knew UNICEF from other postings. Many of their social clubs would invite UNICEF to set up sales stands at their Christmas fairs every year. These included the British Club, German Club, Hollandse Club and Japanese Club. Through the international schools, we were also able to publicise the work of UNICEF. The Overseas Family School, Tanglin Trust School and Canadian International School gave us platforms regularly to talk about the street children of Brazil and the child soldiers of Africa.

In addition, the support for UNICEF in Europe partially continued into Singapore through the European companies that had set up offices here. These companies, such as France's AXA and BNP Paribas, Germany's Allianz and

Siemens, Switzerland's Firmenich and Novartis, Italy's Foster Wheeler and Sweden's Ericsson, were faithful UNICEF customers over many years. Of the Asian companies, the Japanese were particularly supportive. Mitsui and Mitsubishi bought cards, while Isetan department store and Kinokuniya bookstore would stock the cards in their shops during the festive season.

Singaporean companies such as Select Books, Times bookshops, Cold Storage supermarket chain and Table Art Décor also became staunch supporters, taking UNICEF cards on consignment every year for many years.

The role played by volunteers cannot be overstated.[1] We were blessed by the generosity of so many volunteers who gave of their time and talent. Many became and remain friends.

Memorable Media

Today in the age of the Internet, WhatsApp, Twitter, Instagram and YouTube, the role of television, radio and press may be diminished in countries that have high rates of Internet penetration and connectivity. But in the early 1990s, having the mainstream media to help broadcast our messages was critical for our advocacy work. It also helped our credibility in Singapore, where UNICEF was largely unknown at that time and perceived endorsement from entities that held public trust was important. To this end, we were much helped by a range of UNICEF-produced multimedia resources such as videos — some were heart-warming, others heart-rending.

One example was *Meena*, a series of animation programmes that we used to advocate on behalf of the girl child. *Meena* was so successful as a media advocacy tool that there is now an award[2] that builds on this approach of advocacy. It is another example of how new initiatives are constantly being piloted, evolving and being built upon.

Another example was *341*, one of the most unforgettable and affective videos, which never failed to move with its powerful message:

> *… 40,000 a day. A quarter of a million a week. A child every two seconds.*
> *And behind every child who dies, 10 more live on with malnutrition,*
> *unable to grow normally in body or in mind.*

---

[1] See Penny Whitworth's "Civil Society: A Special Relationship" in this volume.
[2] From the UNICEF website: "Introduced in 2005, Meena Media Award has stepped into [its eleventh] year in 2015. The award recognizes excellence in promoting children's issues in the media. The award is named after Meena, the popular animation character created in Bangladesh. Meena is the iconic girl child, a change agent, whose attractive stories champion the rights of children across South Asia."

By any measure, this is the greatest tragedy of our times.
But because it happens every day, it simply isn't news.
No earthquake, no famine, no flood ever killed 40,000 children in a single day.

The figure of 40,000 children a day became more shocking when one was reminded that it was equivalent to 100 aeroplanes crashing in one day, each carrying 400 children, with no survivors.

Over half of the deaths were caused by five common diseases: diarrhoeal dehydration, measles, whooping cough, tetanus and pneumonia. At the corner of the frame, there was a ticking count-up as the video played. In the last frame, the number stops at 341 — the number of children who would have died in the time that it had taken for someone to watch the video.

Today, the number of deaths has gone down. But "as many as 35 million more children could die mostly from preventable causes between 2015 and 2028, if the global community does not take immediate action to accelerate progress."[3] And in 2012, UNICEF and a few partner governments launched *Committing to Child Survival: A Promise Renewed.*[4]

Raising More than Money

Many of the approaches that UNICEF took both in the field and in fundraising achieved more than one objective at a time.

One hugely successful fundraising initiative that achieved multiple objectives was *Change for Good.* Although it had been launched in 1987, it was really in the 1990s that the early adopters among airlines helped the movement to gain momentum and take flight. Collecting the change in different currencies was a brilliant way of raising income for UNICEF. But equally important was the in-flight video that informed passengers of the programme, and the envelopes distributed to collect the change helped to engage and convert new supporters to the cause of children. Although we did not succeed in persuading Singapore Airlines (SIA) to join the programme then, we continue to hope that it will in the future. (A few years later, I was comforted to learn that SIA was using UNICEF greeting cards when I received one from them for my birthday!)

---

[3] See details to UNICEF report: http://www.unicef.org/media/media_70371.html

[4] A Promise Renewed is a global movement that seeks to mobilise and intensify global action to improve the health of women and children around to accelerate reductions in preventable maternal, newborn and child deaths. The movement emerged from the Child Survival Call to Action, a high-level forum convened in June 2012 by the Governments of Ethiopia, India and the United States, in collaboration with UNICEF, to examine ways to spur progress on child survival. See details to UNICEF report: http://www.unicef.org/media/media_70371.html

With email and e-cards today, it is hard to imagine how UNICEF could have raised a substantial amount of money from selling greeting cards; and yet it did. Every year, the cards, gift tags, diaries, jigsaw puzzles and mugs contributed tens of millions of dollars for UNICEF to provide seed-funding to buy, for example, school uniforms and books, carry out immunisation programmes in a worldwide effort to eradicate polio, provide tube-wells in Bangladesh and train art therapists in Macedonia.

But UNICEF cards did not just bring in precious financial resources for programmes for children. They were also messengers and advocacy tools. On the back of each UNICEF card, there would be a message in three or four official United Nations languages about what UNICEF was doing to ensure every child's rights or how vaccination was helping to reduce polio infection rates in the world. So each UNICEF card user had not just made a donation to UNICEF, she or he had also helped UNICEF, literally, to send a message to another potential supporter.

Conclusion

In a small office such as the one in Singapore, there was much variety in the range of projects and tasks. On a Monday morning, there could be appreciation notes to write to volunteers who had helped out at sales stands over the weekend. In the afternoon, the sales stand in a Cold Storage supermarket might have to be replenished because it had been (hopefully) emptied out by the weekend shoppers. The next day, it would be time to design and make copies of a promotional leaflet that might be inserted into IKEA catalogues to be sent out islandwide, or for a meeting with journalists to brief them on the upcoming release of the latest edition of UNICEF's flagship annual publication, *The State of the World's Children* or the *Progress of Nations*. The day after, there would be a review of advocacy videos to select the ones to be shown at the Open House to be held on Saturday.

I never did personally come to know any of the child soldiers from Sierra Leone or any of the children maimed by landmines in El Salvador, but their images on UNICEF posters and photos beseeched us all in the Singapore office to go out and tell their story. They were the reason that staff and volunteers gave up their weekends and after-work evenings to stand for hours approaching strangers to buy a UNICEF mug, calendar or stationery set.

While UNICEF is best known for its milk programme by older Singaporeans, today a whole new generation of Singaporean volunteers and donors has got to know UNICEF, through the UNICEF Greeting Card office in Singapore in the 1980s and 1990s. And through the greeting cards and gifts, exhibitions, talks and videos, they have come to know the children that UNICEF continues to represent, support and protect, seven decades after it started on its mission.

Postscript

Unfortunately, on 9 September 2015, UNICEF confirmed that the Millennium Development Goal (MDG) of a two-third reduction of under-five child mortality would not be met by this year. Although extraordinary progress has been made and under-five deaths have dropped from 12.7 million per year in 1990 to 5.9 million in 2015, it is still not enough to meet the MDG. However, it is encouraging that the figure has dropped below 6 million for the first time.

> *We have to acknowledge tremendous global progress, especially since 2000 when many countries have tripled the rate of reduction of under-five mortality. But the far too large number of children still dying from preventable causes before their fifth birthday — and indeed within their first month of life — should impel us to redouble our efforts to do what we know needs to be done. We cannot continue to fail them.*

UNICEF Deputy Executive Director Geeta Rao Gupta, 9 September 2015

Most child deaths are preventable. Almost half (45%) of under-five deaths occur in the first 28 days of life and are associated with under-nutrition. The leading causes of deaths of children under 5 years old are prematurity, pneumonia, complications during labour and delivery, diarrhoea, sepsis and malaria. The work of UNICEF and its partners continues.

A Practice to Build On

Penny Whitworth

Penny Whitworth, a British national, worked with UNICEF, United Nations Children's Fund, from 1975 to 2008. Her professional experience at UNICEF included postings to Geneva, Singapore and New York. She worked in the Singapore office of UNICEF from 1991–1998. Here she reflects on the power of partnership and collaboration to ensure the rights of every child and make real progress for girls and boys, especially the most disadvantaged and vulnerable.

Almost 70 years after it was created in 1946 as the United Nations International Emergency Fund, UNICEF continues to play a leading role in the global collaborative approaches to humanitarian action. Over the past year, in countries around the world, violent conflicts placed millions of children and their families in danger. Children were bombed in their beds and in their schools, kidnapped, tortured and recruited to fight and kill. Natural and man-made disasters threatened millions more. The largest displacement of people since WWII subjected yet more children to profound deprivation and despair.[1] UNICEF has strengthened its capacity to rapidly deploy specialised staff, direct programmes of protection, education, healthcare, nutrition and operational support by building on and learning from results that help to build a better world for every child and the future we all share.

Today UNICEF is a leading humanitarian and development agency working globally for the rights of every child. Child rights begin with safe shelter, nutrition,

---

[1] See details in *UNICEF Humanitarian Action for Children 2015*, http://www.unicef.org/publications/index_78949.html.

protection from disaster and conflict, and include pre-natal care for healthy births, clean water and sanitation, healthcare and education.

UNICEF has formed a network of relevant, collaborative and voluntary partnerships that have been critical to achieving results for children through innovative programmes and advocacy. The opportunities for engagement are multiple and are a significant factor to maximising development results for children. Due to its longstanding engagement with many partners, UNICEF has been recognised as a leader among United Nations agencies, funds and programmes on partnerships. A 2005 report by Jan Martin Witte and Wolfgang Reinicke, titled *Business UNusual: Facilitating United Nations Reform through Partnerships*, found that UNICEF was "probably the most advanced of all United Nations organisations in integrating partnerships into its core activities."

Several chapters in this book draw attention to the effective collaboration UNICEF has with the corporate sector. A number of contributors have written of their efforts to leverage the strengths of the companies they worked for or their own companies to advance issues vital to children. These partnerships with UNICEF frequently embrace a range of efforts that involve the companies' employees, customers, direct engagement with issues such as child labour in communities within which they operate in addition to cash and in-kind contributions.[2]

The sampling described in this book by the people who were directly involved illustrate how different skills, experience and knowledge have been adjusted and mobilised with governments, institutions, local communities, civil society organisations, the corporate sector, centres of knowledge and research, media, celebrities and other entities.

Over the years, progress for children has been achieved. Perhaps most telling would be in the number of preventable deaths among children under five; this was cut nearly in half between 1990 and 2013. Much remains to be done in a world where in many countries the poorest students receive up to 18 times less public education resources than the wealthiest. On the eve of its 70th anniversary, in the context of what are known as the Sustainable Development Goals that are being developed to plan for human progress over the next 15 years, UNICEF is putting forward an Agenda for every child, girls and boys, especially the most disadvantaged and vulnerable.[3] The 10 points proposed are:

---

[2] See details at http://www.unicef.org/corporate_partners/index_24525.html.
[3] See details in UNICEF's *An Agenda for #EVERYCHILD 2015*, http://www.unicef.org/post2015/index_81485.html.

1. End violence against children
2. Put ending child poverty at the centre of global poverty eradication
3. Renew the global effort to end preventable newborn, child and maternal deaths
4. Pay more attention to adolescence, the second decade of life
5. Leverage the growing "Data Revolution" to support the rights of every child
6. Increase investments in all children, especially the most vulnerable and marginalised
7. Break the cycle of chronic crises affecting children
8. Prioritise education so that all children and adolescents are in school and learning
9. Stop girls being left out, held back and pushed aside
10. Tackle climate change for the sake of future generations

This call to action is one where Singapore and Singaporeans are well placed to augment and engage the expertise, praxis and knowledge required to meet these goals. Fifty years after Singapore gained independence, its children enjoy some of the highest levels of literacy, early childhood education, healthcare and nutrition in the world. The government and people continue to adapt and adopt the best proven solutions based on results and testing that will continue to improve children's lives.

This approach is affirmed throughout this book. Staff, partners and volunteers using their knowledge, practice and networks to solve a particular issue. Consistently key components that emerge to achieve results for children are partnership and collaboration. People struggle with complex issues and new challenges, some feel overwhelmed by the statistics and seemingly never-ending crises and feel numb, some are indignant, all want to be part of the solutions, to take action so that children can survive, develop, be protected and may flourish. Evidence substantiates the collaborative and inclusive practices; we know that little can be resolved in isolation. That is the story of partnership or special relationship that we have chosen to commemorate in this book.

Appendix

Convention on the Rights of the Child

Adopted and opened for signature, ratification and accession by General Assembly resolution 44/25 of 20 November 1989 entry into force 2 September 1990, in accordance with article 49

Preamble

The States Parties to the present Convention,

Considering that, in accordance with the principles proclaimed in the Charter of the United Nations, recognition of the inherent dignity and of the equal and inalienable rights of all members of the human family is the foundation of freedom, justice and peace in the world,

Bearing in mind that the peoples of the United Nations have, in the Charter, reaffirmed their faith in fundamental human rights and in the dignity and worth of the human person, and have determined to promote social progress and better standards of life in larger freedom,

Recognizing that the United Nations has, in the Universal Declaration of Human Rights and in the International Covenants on Human Rights, proclaimed and agreed that everyone is entitled to all the rights and freedoms set forth therein, without distinction of any kind, such as race, colour, sex, language, religion, political or other opinion, national or social origin, property, birth or other status,

Recalling that, in the Universal Declaration of Human Rights, the United Nations has proclaimed that childhood is entitled to special care and assistance,

Convinced that the family, as the fundamental group of society and the natural environment for the growth and well-being of all its members and particularly children, should be afforded the necessary protection and assistance so that it can fully assume its responsibilities within the community,

Recognizing that the child, for the full and harmonious development of his or her personality, should grow up in a family environment, in an atmosphere of happiness, love and understanding,

Considering that the child should be fully prepared to live an individual life in society, and brought up in the spirit of the ideals proclaimed in the Charter of the United Nations, and in particular in the spirit of peace, dignity, tolerance, freedom, equality and solidarity,

Bearing in mind that the need to extend particular care to the child has been stated in the Geneva Declaration of the Rights of the Child of 1924 and in the Declaration of the Rights of the Child adopted by the General Assembly on 20 November 1959 and recognized in the Universal Declaration of Human Rights, in the International Covenant on Civil and Political Rights (in particular in articles 23 and 24), in the International Covenant on Economic, Social and Cultural Rights (in particular in article 10) and in the statutes and relevant instruments of specialized agencies and international organizations concerned with the welfare of children,

Bearing in mind that, as indicated in the Declaration of the Rights of the Child, "the child, by reason of his physical and mental immaturity, needs special safeguards and care, including appropriate legal protection, before as well as after birth",

Recalling the provisions of the Declaration on Social and Legal Principles relating to the Protection and Welfare of Children, with Special Reference to Foster Placement and Adoption Nationally and Internationally; the United Nations Standard Minimum Rules for the Administration of Juvenile Justice (The Beijing Rules); and the Declaration on the Protection of Women and Children in Emergency and Armed Conflict, Recognizing that, in all countries in the world, there are children living in exceptionally difficult conditions, and that such children need special consideration,

Taking due account of the importance of the traditions and cultural values of each people for the protection and harmonious development of the child, Recognizing the importance of international co-operation for improving the living conditions of children in every country, in particular in the developing countries,

Have agreed as follows:

PART I

Article 1

For the purposes of the present Convention, a child means every human being below the age of eighteen years unless under the law applicable to the child, majority is attained earlier.

Article 2

1. States Parties shall respect and ensure the rights set forth in the present Convention to each child within their jurisdiction without discrimination of any kind, irrespective of the child's or his or her parent's or legal guardian's race, colour, sex, language, religion, political or other opinion, national, ethnic or social origin, property, disability, birth or other status.
2. States Parties shall take all appropriate measures to ensure that the child is protected against all forms of discrimination or punishment on the basis of the status, activities, expressed opinions, or beliefs of the child's parents, legal guardians, or family members.

Article 3

1. In all actions concerning children, whether undertaken by public or private social welfare institutions, courts of law, administrative authorities or legislative bodies, the best interests of the child shall be a primary consideration.
2. States Parties undertake to ensure the child such protection and care as is necessary for his or her well-being, taking into account the rights and duties of his or her parents, legal guardians, or other individuals legally responsible for him or her, and, to this end, shall take all appropriate legislative and administrative measures.
3. States Parties shall ensure that the institutions, services and facilities responsible for the care or protection of children shall conform with the standards established by competent authorities, particularly in the areas of safety, health, in the number and suitability of their staff, as well as competent supervision.

Article 4

States Parties shall undertake all appropriate legislative, administrative, and other measures for the implementation of the rights recognized in the present Convention. With regard to economic, social and cultural rights, States Parties shall undertake such measures to the maximum extent of their available resources and, where needed, within the framework of international co-operation.

Article 5

States Parties shall respect the responsibilities, rights and duties of parents or, where applicable, the members of the extended family or community as provided for by local custom, legal guardians or other persons legally responsible for the child, to provide, in a manner consistent with the evolving capacities of the child, appropriate direction and guidance in the exercise by the child of the rights recognized in the present Convention.

Article 6

1. States Parties recognize that every child has the inherent right to life.
2. States Parties shall ensure to the maximum extent possible the survival and development of the child.

Article 7

1. The child shall be registered immediately after birth and shall have the right from birth to a name, the right to acquire a nationality and. as far as possible, the right to know and be cared for by his or her parents.
2. States Parties shall ensure the implementation of these rights in accordance with their national law and their obligations under the relevant international instruments in this field, in particular where the child would otherwise be stateless.

Article 8

1. States Parties undertake to respect the right of the child to preserve his or her identity, including nationality, name and family relations as recognized by law without unlawful interference.
2. Where a child is illegally deprived of some or all of the elements of his or her identity, States Parties shall provide appropriate assistance and protection, with a view to re-establishing speedily his or her identity.

Article 9

1. States Parties shall ensure that a child shall not be separated from his or her parents against their will, except when competent authorities subject to judicial review determine, in accordance with applicable law and procedures, that such separation is necessary for the best interests of the child. Such determination may be necessary in a particular case such as one involving abuse or neglect of the child by the parents, or one where the parents are living separately and a decision must be made as to the child's place of residence.

2. In any proceedings pursuant to paragraph 1 of the present article, all interested parties shall be given an opportunity to participate in the proceedings and make their views known.

3. States Parties shall respect the right of the child who is separated from one or both parents to maintain personal relations and direct contact with both parents on a regular basis, except if it is contrary to the child's best interests.

4. Where such separation results from any action initiated by a State Party, such as the detention, imprisonment, exile, deportation or death (including death arising from any cause while the person is in the custody of the State) of one or both parents or of the child, that State Party shall, upon request, provide the parents, the child or, if appropriate, another member of the family with the essential information concerning the whereabouts of the absent member(s) of the family unless the provision of the information would be detrimental to the well-being of the child. States Parties shall further ensure that the submission of such a request shall of itself entail no adverse consequences for the person(s) concerned.

Article 10

1. In accordance with the obligation of States Parties under article 9, paragraph 1, applications by a child or his or her parents to enter or leave a State Party for the purpose of family reunification shall be dealt with by States Parties in a positive, humane and expeditious manner. States Parties shall further ensure that the submission of such a request shall entail no adverse consequences for the applicants and for the members of their family.

2. A child whose parents reside in different States shall have the right to maintain on a regular basis, save in exceptional circumstances personal relations and direct contacts with both parents. Towards that end and in accordance with the obligation of States Parties under article 9, paragraph 1, States Parties shall respect the right of the child and his or her parents to leave any country, including their own, and to enter their own country. The right to leave any country shall be subject only to such restrictions as are prescribed by law and which are necessary to protect the national security, public order (ordre public), public health or morals or the rights and freedoms of others and are consistent with the other rights recognized in the present Convention.

Article 11

1. States Parties shall take measures to combat the illicit transfer and non-return of children abroad.

2. To this end, States Parties shall promote the conclusion of bilateral or multilateral agreements or accession to existing agreements.

Article 12

1. States Parties shall assure to the child who is capable of forming his or her own views the right to express those views freely in all matters affecting the child, the views of the child being given due weight in accordance with the age and maturity of the child.
2. For this purpose, the child shall in particular be provided the opportunity to be heard in any judicial and administrative proceedings affecting the child, either directly, or through a representative or an appropriate body, in a manner consistent with the procedural rules of national law.

Article 13

1. The child shall have the right to freedom of expression; this right shall include freedom to seek, receive and impart information and ideas of all kinds, regardless of frontiers, either orally, in writing or in print, in the form of art, or through any other media of the child's choice.
2. The exercise of this right may be subject to certain restrictions, but these shall only be such as are provided by law and are necessary:

   (a) For respect of the rights or reputations of others; or
   (b) For the protection of national security or of public order (ordre public), or of public health or morals.

Article 14

1. States Parties shall respect the right of the child to freedom of thought, conscience and religion.
2. States Parties shall respect the rights and duties of the parents and, when applicable, legal guardians, to provide direction to the child in the exercise of his or her right in a manner consistent with the evolving capacities of the child.
3. Freedom to manifest one's religion or beliefs may be subject only to such limitations as are prescribed by law and are necessary to protect public safety, order, health or morals, or the fundamental rights and freedoms of others.

Article 15

1. States Parties recognize the rights of the child to freedom of association and to freedom of peaceful assembly.
2. No restrictions may be placed on the exercise of these rights other than those imposed in conformity with the law and which are necessary in a democratic society in the interests of national security or public safety, public order (ordre public), the protection of public health or morals or the protection of the rights and freedoms of others.

Article 16

1. No child shall be subjected to arbitrary or unlawful interference with his or her privacy, family, or correspondence, nor to unlawful attacks on his or her honour and reputation.
2. The child has the right to the protection of the law against such interference or attacks.

Article 17

States Parties recognize the important function performed by the mass media and shall ensure that the child has access to information and material from a diversity of national and international sources, especially those aimed at the promotion of his or her social, spiritual and moral well-being and physical and mental health.

To this end, States Parties shall:

(a) Encourage the mass media to disseminate information and material of social and cultural benefit to the child and in accordance with the spirit of article 29;
(b) Encourage international co-operation in the production, exchange and dissemination of such information and material from a diversity of cultural, national and international sources;
(c) Encourage the production and dissemination of children's books;
(d) Encourage the mass media to have particular regard to the linguistic needs of the child who belongs to a minority group or who is indigenous;
(e) Encourage the development of appropriate guidelines for the protection of the child from information and material injurious to his or her well-being, bearing in mind the provisions of articles 13 and 18.

Article 18

1. States Parties shall use their best efforts to ensure recognition of the principle that both parents have common responsibilities for the upbringing and development of the child. Parents or, as the case may be, legal guardians, have the primary responsibility for the upbringing and development of the child. The best interests of the child will be their basic concern.
2. For the purpose of guaranteeing and promoting the rights set forth in the present Convention, States Parties shall render appropriate assistance to parents and legal guardians in the performance of their child-rearing responsibilities and shall ensure the development of institutions, facilities and services for the care of children.
3. States Parties shall take all appropriate measures to ensure that children of working parents have the right to benefit from child-care services and facilities for which they are eligible.

Article 19

1. States Parties shall take all appropriate legislative, administrative, social and educational measures to protect the child from all forms of physical or mental violence, injury or abuse, neglect or negligent treatment, maltreatment or exploitation, including sexual abuse, while in the care of parent(s), legal guardian(s) or any other person who has the care of the child.
2. Such protective measures should, as appropriate, include effective procedures for the establishment of social programmes to provide necessary support for the child and for those who have the care of the child, as well as for other forms of prevention and for identification, reporting, referral, investigation, treatment and follow-up of instances of child maltreatment described heretofore, and, as appropriate, for judicial involvement.

Article 20

1. A child temporarily or permanently deprived of his or her family environment, or in whose own best interests cannot be allowed to remain in that environment, shall be entitled to special protection and assistance provided by the State.
2. States Parties shall in accordance with their national laws ensure alternative care for such a child.
3. Such care could include, inter alia, foster placement, kafalah of Islamic law, adoption or if necessary placement in suitable institutions for the care of children. When considering solutions, due regard shall be paid to the desirability of continuity in a child's upbringing and to the child's ethnic, religious, cultural and linguistic background.

Article 21

States Parties that recognize and/or permit the system of adoption shall ensure that the best interests of the child shall be the paramount consideration and they shall:

(a) Ensure that the adoption of a child is authorized only by competent authorities who determine, in accordance with applicable law and procedures and on the basis of all pertinent and reliable information, that the adoption is permissible in view of the child's status concerning parents, relatives and legal guardians and that, if required, the persons concerned have given their informed consent to the adoption on the basis of such counselling as may be necessary;

(b) Recognize that inter-country adoption may be considered as an alternative means of child's care, if the child cannot be placed in a foster or an adoptive family or cannot in any suitable manner be cared for in the child's country of origin;

(c) Ensure that the child concerned by inter-country adoption enjoys safeguards and standards equivalent to those existing in the case of national adoption;

(d) Take all appropriate measures to ensure that, in inter-country adoption, the placement does not result in improper financial gain for those involved in it;

(e) Promote, where appropriate, the objectives of the present article by concluding bilateral or multilateral arrangements or agreements, and endeavour, within this framework, to ensure that the placement of the child in another country is carried out by competent authorities or organs.

Article 22

1. States Parties shall take appropriate measures to ensure that a child who is seeking refugee status or who is considered a refugee in accordance with applicable international or domestic law and procedures shall, whether unaccompanied or accompanied by his or her parents or by any other person, receive appropriate protection and humanitarian assistance in the enjoyment of applicable rights set forth in the present Convention and in other international human rights or humanitarian instruments to which the said States are Parties.

2. For this purpose, States Parties shall provide, as they consider appropriate, co-operation in any efforts by the United Nations and other competent intergovernmental organizations or non-governmental organizations co-operating with the United Nations to protect and assist such a child and to trace the parents or other members of the family of any refugee child in order to obtain information necessary for reunification with his or her family. In cases where no parents or other members of the family can be found, the child shall be accorded the same protection as any other child permanently or temporarily deprived of his or her family environment for any reason , as set forth in the present Convention.

Article 23

1. States Parties recognize that a mentally or physically disabled child should enjoy a full and decent life, in conditions which ensure dignity, promote self-reliance and facilitate the child's active participation in the community.

2. States Parties recognize the right of the disabled child to special care and shall encourage and ensure the extension, subject to available resources, to the eligible child and those responsible for his or her care, of assistance for which application is made and which is appropriate to the child's condition and to the circumstances of the parents or others caring for the child.

3. Recognizing the special needs of a disabled child, assistance extended in accordance with paragraph 2 of the present article shall be provided free of

charge, whenever possible, taking into account the financial resources of the parents or others caring for the child, and shall be designed to ensure that the disabled child has effective access to and receives education, training, health care services, rehabilitation services, preparation for employment and recreation opportunities in a manner conducive to the child's achieving the fullest possible social integration and individual development, including his or her cultural and spiritual development.

4. States Parties shall promote, in the spirit of international cooperation, the exchange of appropriate information in the field of preventive health care and of medical, psychological and functional treatment of disabled children, including dissemination of and access to information concerning methods of rehabilitation, education and vocational services, with the aim of enabling States Parties to improve their capabilities and skills and to widen their experience in these areas. In this regard, particular account shall be taken of the needs of developing countries.

Article 24

1. States Parties recognize the right of the child to the enjoyment of the highest attainable standard of health and to facilities for the treatment of illness and rehabilitation of health. States Parties shall strive to ensure that no child is deprived of his or her right of access to such health care services.

2. States Parties shall pursue full implementation of this right and, in particular, shall take appropriate measures:

    (a) To diminish infant and child mortality;
    (b) To ensure the provision of necessary medical assistance and health care to all children with emphasis on the development of primary health care;
    (c) To combat disease and malnutrition, including within the framework of primary health care, through, inter alia, the application of readily available technology and through the provision of adequate nutritious foods and clean drinking-water, taking into consideration the dangers and risks of environmental pollution;
    (d) To ensure appropriate pre-natal and post-natal health care for mothers;
    (e) To ensure that all segments of society, in particular parents and children, are informed, have access to education and are supported in the use of basic knowledge of child health and nutrition, the advantages of breast-feeding, hygiene and environmental sanitation and the prevention of accidents;
    (f) To develop preventive health care, guidance for parents and family planning education and services.

3. States Parties shall take all effective and appropriate measures with a view to abolishing traditional practices prejudicial to the health of children.

4. States Parties undertake to promote and encourage international co-operation with a view to achieving progressively the full realization of the right recognized in the present article. In this regard, particular account shall be taken of the needs of developing countries.

Article 25

States Parties recognize the right of a child who has been placed by the competent authorities for the purposes of care, protection or treatment of his or her physical or mental health, to a periodic review of the treatment provided to the child and all other circumstances relevant to his or her placement.

Article 26

1. States Parties shall recognize for every child the right to benefit from social security, including social insurance, and shall take the necessary measures to achieve the full realization of this right in accordance with their national law.

2. The benefits should, where appropriate, be granted, taking into account the resources and the circumstances of the child and persons having responsibility for the maintenance of the child, as well as any other consideration relevant to an application for benefits made by or on behalf of the child.

Article 27

1. States Parties recognize the right of every child to a standard of living adequate for the child's physical, mental, spiritual, moral and social development.

2. The parent(s) or others responsible for the child have the primary responsibility to secure, within their abilities and financial capacities, the conditions of living necessary for the child's development.

3. States Parties, in accordance with national conditions and within their means, shall take appropriate measures to assist parents and others responsible for the child to implement this right and shall in case of need provide material assistance and support programmes, particularly with regard to nutrition, clothing and housing.

4. States Parties shall take all appropriate measures to secure the recovery of maintenance for the child from the parents or other persons having financial responsibility for the child, both within the State Party and from abroad. In particular, where the person having financial responsibility for the child lives in a State different from that of the child, States Parties shall promote the accession to international agreements or the conclusion of such agreements, as well as the making of other appropriate arrangements.

Article 28

1. States Parties recognize the right of the child to education, and with a view to achieving this right progressively and on the basis of equal opportunity, they shall, in particular:

   (a) Make primary education compulsory and available free to all;
   (b) Encourage the development of different forms of secondary education, including general and vocational education, make them available and accessible to every child, and take appropriate measures such as the introduction of free education and offering financial assistance in case of need;
   (c) Make higher education accessible to all on the basis of capacity by every appropriate means;
   (d) Make educational and vocational information and guidance available and accessible to all children;
   (e) Take measures to encourage regular attendance at schools and the reduction of drop-out rates.

2. States Parties shall take all appropriate measures to ensure that school discipline is administered in a manner consistent with the child's human dignity and in conformity with the present Convention.

3. States Parties shall promote and encourage international cooperation in matters relating to education, in particular with a view to contributing to the elimination of ignorance and illiteracy throughout the world and facilitating access to scientific and technical knowledge and modern teaching methods. In this regard, particular account shall be taken of the needs of developing countries.

Article 29

1. States Parties agree that the education of the child shall be directed to:

   (a) The development of the child's personality, talents and mental and physical abilities to their fullest potential;
   (b) The development of respect for human rights and fundamental freedoms, and for the principles enshrined in the Charter of the United Nations;
   (c) The development of respect for the child's parents, his or her own cultural identity, language and values, for the national values of the country in which the child is living, the country from which he or she may originate, and for civilizations different from his or her own;
   (d) The preparation of the child for responsible life in a free society, in the spirit of understanding, peace, tolerance, equality of sexes, and friendship

among all peoples, ethnic, national and religious groups and persons of indigenous origin;

(e) The development of respect for the natural environment.

2. No part of the present article or article 28 shall be construed so as to interfere with the liberty of individuals and bodies to establish and direct educational institutions, subject always to the observance of the principle set forth in paragraph 1 of the present article and to the requirements that the education given in such institutions shall conform to such minimum standards as may be laid down by the State.

Article 30

In those States in which ethnic, religious or linguistic minorities or persons of indigenous origin exist, a child belonging to such a minority or who is indigenous shall not be denied the right, in community with other members of his or her group, to enjoy his or her own culture, to profess and practise his or her own religion, or to use his or her own language.

Article 31

1. States Parties recognize the right of the child to rest and leisure, to engage in play and recreational activities appropriate to the age of the child and to participate freely in cultural life and the arts.
2. States Parties shall respect and promote the right of the child to participate fully in cultural and artistic life and shall encourage the provision of appropriate and equal opportunities for cultural, artistic, recreational and leisure activity.

Article 32

1. States Parties recognize the right of the child to be protected from economic exploitation and from performing any work that is likely to be hazardous or to interfere with the child's education, or to be harmful to the child's health or physical, mental, spiritual, moral or social development.
2. States Parties shall take legislative, administrative, social and educational measures to ensure the implementation of the present article. To this end, and having regard to the relevant provisions of other international instruments, States Parties shall in particular:

   (a) Provide for a minimum age or minimum ages for admission to employment;
   (b) Provide for appropriate regulation of the hours and conditions of employment;

(c) Provide for appropriate penalties or other sanctions to ensure the effective enforcement of the present article.

Article 33

States Parties shall take all appropriate measures, including legislative, administrative, social and educational measures, to protect children from the illicit use of narcotic drugs and psychotropic substances as defined in the relevant international treaties, and to prevent the use of children in the illicit production and trafficking of such substances.

Article 34

States Parties undertake to protect the child from all forms of sexual exploitation and sexual abuse. For these purposes, States Parties shall in particular take all appropriate national, bilateral and multilateral measures to prevent:

(a) The inducement or coercion of a child to engage in any unlawful sexual activity;
(b) The exploitative use of children in prostitution or other unlawful sexual practices;
(c) The exploitative use of children in pornographic performances and materials.

Article 35

States Parties shall take all appropriate national, bilateral and multilateral measures to prevent the abduction of, the sale of or traffic in children for any purpose or in any form.

Article 36

States Parties shall protect the child against all other forms of exploitation prejudicial to any aspects of the child's welfare.

Article 37

States Parties shall ensure that:

(a) No child shall be subjected to torture or other cruel, inhuman or degrading treatment or punishment. Neither capital punishment nor life imprisonment without possibility of release shall be imposed for offences committed by persons below eighteen years of age;
(b) No child shall be deprived of his or her liberty unlawfully or arbitrarily. The arrest, detention or imprisonment of a child shall be in conformity with the

law and shall be used only as a measure of last resort and for the shortest appropriate period of time;

(c) Every child deprived of liberty shall be treated with humanity and respect for the inherent dignity of the human person, and in a manner which takes into account the needs of persons of his or her age. In particular, every child deprived of liberty shall be separated from adults unless it is considered in the child's best interest not to do so and shall have the right to maintain contact with his or her family through correspondence and visits, save in exceptional circumstances;

(d) Every child deprived of his or her liberty shall have the right to prompt access to legal and other appropriate assistance, as well as the right to challenge the legality of the deprivation of his or her liberty before a court or other competent, independent and impartial authority, and to a prompt decision on any such action.

Article 38

1. States Parties undertake to respect and to ensure respect for rules of international humanitarian law applicable to them in armed conflicts which are relevant to the child.

2. States Parties shall take all feasible measures to ensure that persons who have not attained the age of fifteen years do not take a direct part in hostilities.

3. States Parties shall refrain from recruiting any person who has not attained the age of fifteen years into their armed forces. In recruiting among those persons who have attained the age of fifteen years but who have not attained the age of eighteen years, States Parties shall endeavour to give priority to those who are oldest.

4. In accordance with their obligations under international humanitarian law to protect the civilian population in armed conflicts, States Parties shall take all feasible measures to ensure protection and care of children who are affected by an armed conflict.

Article 39

States Parties shall take all appropriate measures to promote physical and psychological recovery and social reintegration of a child victim of: any form of neglect, exploitation, or abuse; torture or any other form of cruel, inhuman or degrading treatment or punishment; or armed conflicts. Such recovery and reintegration shall take place in an environment which fosters the health, self-respect and dignity of the child.

Article 40

1. States Parties recognize the right of every child alleged as, accused of, or recognized as having infringed the penal law to be treated in a manner consistent with the promotion of the child's sense of dignity and worth, which reinforces the child's respect for the human rights and fundamental freedoms of others and which takes into account the child's age and the desirability of promoting the child's reintegration and the child's assuming a constructive role in society.

2. To this end, and having regard to the relevant provisions of international instruments, States Parties shall, in particular, ensure that:

    (a) No child shall be alleged as, be accused of, or recognized as having infringed the penal law by reason of acts or omissions that were not prohibited by national or international law at the time they were committed;

    (b) Every child alleged as or accused of having infringed the penal law has at least the following guarantees:

        (i) To be presumed innocent until proven guilty according to law;

        (ii) To be informed promptly and directly of the charges against him or her, and, if appropriate, through his or her parents or legal guardians, and to have legal or other appropriate assistance in the preparation and presentation of his or her defence;

        (iii) To have the matter determined without delay by a competent, independent and impartial authority or judicial body in a fair hearing according to law, in the presence of legal or other appropriate assistance and, unless it is considered not to be in the best interest of the child, in particular, taking into account his or her age or situation, his or her parents or legal guardians;

        (iv) Not to be compelled to give testimony or to confess guilt; to examine or have examined adverse witnesses and to obtain the participation and examination of witnesses on his or her behalf under conditions of equality;

        (v) If considered to have infringed the penal law, to have this decision and any measures imposed in consequence thereof reviewed by a higher competent, independent and impartial authority or judicial body according to law;

        (vi) To have the free assistance of an interpreter if the child cannot understand or speak the language used;

> (vii) To have his or her privacy fully respected at all stages of the proceedings.

3. States Parties shall seek to promote the establishment of laws, procedures, authorities and institutions specifically applicable to children alleged as, accused of, or recognized as having infringed the penal law, and, in particular:

(a) The establishment of a minimum age below which children shall be presumed not to have the capacity to infringe the penal law;

(b) Whenever appropriate and desirable, measures for dealing with such children without resorting to judicial proceedings, providing that human rights and legal safeguards are fully respected. 4. A variety of dispositions, such as care, guidance and supervision orders; counselling; probation; foster care; education and vocational training programmes and other alternatives to institutional care shall be available to ensure that children are dealt with in a manner appropriate to their well-being and proportionate both to their circumstances and the offence.

Article 41

Nothing in the present Convention shall affect any provisions which are more conducive to the realization of the rights of the child and which may be contained in:

(a) The law of a State party; or
(b) International law in force for that State.

PART II

Article 42

States Parties undertake to make the principles and provisions of the Convention widely known, by appropriate and active means, to adults and children alike.

Article 43

1. For the purpose of examining the progress made by States Parties in achieving the realization of the obligations undertaken in the present Convention, there shall be established a Committee on the Rights of the Child, which shall carry out the functions hereinafter provided.

2. The Committee shall consist of eighteen experts of high moral standing and recognized competence in the field covered by this Convention.1/The members of the Committee shall be elected by States Parties from among their nationals and shall serve in their personal capacity, consideration being given to equitable geographical distribution, as well as to the principal legal systems.

3. The members of the Committee shall be elected by secret ballot from a list of persons nominated by States Parties. Each State Party may nominate one person from among its own nationals.

4. The initial election to the Committee shall be held no later than six months after the date of the entry into force of the present Convention and thereafter every second year. At least four months before the date of each election, the Secretary-General of the United Nations shall address a letter to States Parties inviting them to submit their nominations within two months. The Secretary-General shall subsequently prepare a list in alphabetical order of all persons thus nominated, indicating States Parties which have nominated them, and shall submit it to the States Parties to the present Convention.

5. The elections shall be held at meetings of States Parties convened by the Secretary-General at United Nations Headquarters. At those meetings, for which two thirds of States Parties shall constitute a quorum, the persons elected to the Committee shall be those who obtain the largest number of votes and an absolute majority of the votes of the representatives of States Parties present and voting.

6. The members of the Committee shall be elected for a term of four years. They shall be eligible for re-election if renominated. The term of five of the members elected at the first election shall expire at the end of two years; immediately after the first election, the names of these five members shall be chosen by lot by the Chairman of the meeting.

7. If a member of the Committee dies or resigns or declares that for any other cause he or she can no longer perform the duties of the Committee, the State Party which nominated the member shall appoint another expert from among its nationals to serve for the remainder of the term, subject to the approval of the Committee.

8. The Committee shall establish its own rules of procedure.

9. The Committee shall elect its officers for a period of two years.

10. The meetings of the Committee shall normally be held at United Nations Headquarters or at any other convenient place as determined by the Committee. The Committee shall normally meet annually. The duration of the meetings of the Committee shall be determined, and reviewed, if necessary, by a meeting of the States Parties to the present Convention, subject to the approval of the General Assembly.

11. The Secretary-General of the United Nations shall provide the necessary staff and facilities for the effective performance of the functions of the Committee under the present Convention.

12. With the approval of the General Assembly, the members of the Committee established under the present Convention shall receive emoluments from United Nations resources on such terms and conditions as the Assembly may decide.

Article 44

1. States Parties undertake to submit to the Committee, through the Secretary-General of the United Nations, reports on the measures they have adopted which give effect to the rights recognized herein and on the progress made on the enjoyment of those rights

    (a) Within two years of the entry into force of the Convention for the State Party concerned;
    (b) Thereafter every five years.

2. Reports made under the present article shall indicate factors and difficulties, if any, affecting the degree of fulfilment of the obligations under the present Convention. Reports shall also contain sufficient information to provide the Committee with a comprehensive understanding of the implementation of the Convention in the country concerned.

3. A State Party which has submitted a comprehensive initial report to the Committee need not, in its subsequent reports submitted in accordance with paragraph 1 (b) of the present article, repeat basic information previously provided.

4. The Committee may request from States Parties further information relevant to the implementation of the Convention.

5. The Committee shall submit to the General Assembly, through the Economic and Social Council, every two years, reports on its activities.

6. States Parties shall make their reports widely available to the public in their own countries.

Article 45

In order to foster the effective implementation of the Convention and to encourage international co-operation in the field covered by the Convention:

(a) The specialized agencies, the United Nations Children's Fund, and other United Nations organs shall be entitled to be represented at the consideration of the implementation of such provisions of the present Convention as fall within the scope of their mandate. The Committee may invite the specialized agencies, the United Nations Children's Fund and other competent bodies as it may consider appropriate to provide expert advice on the implementation of the Convention in areas falling within the scope of their respective mandates. The Committee may invite the specialized agencies, the United Nations Children's Fund, and other United Nations organs to submit reports on the implementation of the Convention in areas falling within the scope of their activities;

(b) The Committee shall transmit, as it may consider appropriate, to the specialized agencies, the United Nations Children's Fund and other competent bodies, any reports from States Parties that contain a request, or indicate a need, for technical advice or assistance, along with the Committee's observations and suggestions, if any, on these requests or indications;

(c) The Committee may recommend to the General Assembly to request the Secretary-General to undertake on its behalf studies on specific issues relating to the rights of the child;

(d) The Committee may make suggestions and general recommendations based on information received pursuant to articles 44 and 45 of the present Convention. Such suggestions and general recommendations shall be transmitted to any State Party concerned and reported to the General Assembly, together with comments, if any, from States Parties.

PART III

Article 46

The present Convention shall be open for signature by all States.

Article 47

The present Convention is subject to ratification. Instruments of ratification shall be deposited with the Secretary-General of the United Nations.

Article 48

The present Convention shall remain open for accession by any State. The instruments of accession shall be deposited with the Secretary-General of the United Nations.

Article 49

1. The present Convention shall enter into force on the thirtieth day following the date of deposit with the Secretary-General of the United Nations of the twentieth instrument of ratification or accession.

2. For each State ratifying or acceding to the Convention after the deposit of the twentieth instrument of ratification or accession, the Convention shall enter into force on the thirtieth day after the deposit by such State of its instrument of ratification or accession.

Article 50

1. Any State Party may propose an amendment and file it with the Secretary-General of the United Nations. The Secretary-General shall thereupon communicate the proposed amendment to States Parties, with a request that they

indicate whether they favour a conference of States Parties for the purpose of considering and voting upon the proposals. In the event that, within four months from the date of such communication, at least one third of the States Parties favour such a conference, the Secretary-General shall convene the conference under the auspices of the United Nations. Any amendment adopted by a majority of States Parties present and voting at the conference shall be submitted to the General Assembly for approval.

2. An amendment adopted in accordance with paragraph 1 of the present article shall enter into force when it has been approved by the General Assembly of the United Nations and accepted by a two-thirds majority of States Parties.

3. When an amendment enters into force, it shall be binding on those States Parties which have accepted it, other States Parties still being bound by the provisions of the present Convention and any earlier amendments which they have accepted.

Article 51

1. The Secretary-General of the United Nations shall receive and circulate to all States the text of reservations made by States at the time of ratification or accession.

2. A reservation incompatible with the object and purpose of the present Convention shall not be permitted.

3. Reservations may be withdrawn at any time by notification to that effect addressed to the Secretary-General of the United Nations, who shall then inform all States. Such notification shall take effect on the date on which it is received by the Secretary-General.

Article 52

A State Party may denounce the present Convention by written notification to the Secretary-General of the United Nations. Denunciation becomes effective one year after the date of receipt of the notification by the Secretary-General.

Article 53

The Secretary-General of the United Nations is designated as the depositary of the present Convention.

Article 54

The original of the present Convention, of which the Arabic, Chinese, English, French, Russian and Spanish texts are equally authentic, shall be deposited with the Secretary-General of the United Nations. In witness thereof the undersigned plenipotentiaries, being duly authorized thereto by their respective Governments, have signed the present Convention.

————————

1/The General Assembly, in its resolution 50/155 of 21 December 1995 , approved the amendment to article 43, paragraph 2, of the Convention on the Rights of the Child, replacing the word "ten" with the word "eighteen". The amendment entered into force on 18 November 2002 when it had been accepted by a two-thirds majority of the States parties (128 out of 191).

About the Editors

Peggy Kek

Peggy Kek is a Singaporean. Her first assignment as Sales Development Assistant in 1991 with UNICEF, United Nations Children's Fund, Greeting Card Operation office in Singapore, led to a lifelong admiration for and relationship with the organisation. She was appointed Assistant Fundraising Officer in 1993 and went on to become a consultant to the UNICEF offices in Vietnam and China.

Over the years she has returned time and time again to serve the organisation — in 2002, 2008, and most recently again in 2012 as Consultant to the UNICEF Regional Office for East Asia and the Pacific (EAPRO) in Bangkok. In the course of her varied assignments, she has worked on fundraising drives, advocacy campaigns, and partnership alliances and interactions that have brought her into contact with many inspiring colleagues, volunteers, businesses, government counterparts and civil society organisations.

Her experiences with UNICEF led her to similar roles in other development agencies including The World Bank (in Washington DC) and The Asia Foundation. Educated in Singapore and the United Kingdom, she fervently believes in the power and importance of partnerships to achieve greater public good, and has continued to build collaborative relationships in her roles at the Asia-Europe Foundation, Institute of Policy Studies, Singapore International Foundation and most recently, at the National University of Singapore.

She is delighted to see this book, a cherished dream, become reality, as a result of renewed collaboration and connection with some with whom she has worked in the past.

Penny Whitworth

Penny Whitworth, a British national, worked with UNICEF, United Nations Children's Fund, from 1975 to 2008. Her professional experience at UNICEF in Geneva, Singapore and New York involved international fundraising and resource mobilisation; building working relationships and negotiating between national and international constituencies in the non-profit and private sectors; corporate social responsibility; leveraging limited resources; communicating key messages, using marketing and logistics experience to identify cross-sectoral solutions and cultivating high net worth donors.

She worked in the Singapore office of UNICEF from 1991–1998. From 1991–1994 she supervised the production and distribution of UNICEF cards, gifts and catalogues for the Asia and Pacific regions; and oversaw product sales, fundraising, information and advocacy campaigns in Singapore. In 1994 she became UNICEF's executive focal point for the development, design, planning and operational management of UNICEF card and product marketing strategies and sales activities in Asia. She considers the founding of a group of active, diverse and enthusiastic volunteers one of her happiest achievements in Singapore.

She lives in New York and currently provides strategic support for Project Continua, an initiative dedicated to the creation and preservation of women's intellectual history. She recently volunteered on after-school programmes with the East Harlem Tutorial Program and the Fresh Air Fund.

Selected Bibliography

Black, M. (1986). *The Children and the Nations: The Story of UNICEF*. New York: UNICEF.

Black, M. (1996). *Children First: The Story of UNICEF, Past and Present*. Oxford: Oxford University Press.

Foo, L. L., Quek, S. J. S., Ng, S. A., Lim, M. T., & Deurenberg-Yap, M. (2005). Breastfeeding Prevalence and Practices Among Singaporean Chinese, Malay and Indian Mothers. *Health Promotion International, 20*(3), 229–237.

Loh, J., & Cheng, D. (2002). *Memoirs of Tay Bak Koi*. Singapore: Eagle's Eye Art Gallery.

Ministry of Health, Singapore. (2015, August). Population and Vital Statistics. Retrieved from https://www.moh.gov.sg/content/moh_web/home/statistics/Health_Facts_Singapore/Population_And_Vital_Statistics.html.

Quek, T. K. (2010). *30 Art Friends: Collecting Southeast Asian Art*. Singapore: Gatehouse Publishing.

UNICEF. (1961). Bulletin of the United Nations Children's Fund, vol. 9, no. 3.

UNICEF. (2006). *1946–2006: Sixty Years for Children*. New York: UNICEF.

UNICEF. (2014, November). *The State of the World's Children 2015: Executive Summary — Reimagine the Future*. New York: UNICEF.

UNICEF. (2015, June). *Progress for Children Beyond Averages: Learning from the MDGs* (11th edition). New York: UNICEF.

UNICEF. Annual Reports, 1972–1999. Retrieved from http://www.unicef.org/about/history/index_annualreports.html.

UNICEF. Annual Reports, 2000–2014. Retrieved from http://www.unicef.org/publications.

United Nations Global Compact. (2005). *Business UNusual: Facilitating United Nations reform through partnerships*. Berlin: Global Public Policy Institute.

UNICEF Statistics & Monitoring Section/Division of Policy and Strategy. (2013, February 26). Progress toward the Millennium Development Goals and other measures of the well-being of children and women: Singapore. Retrieved from http://www.unicef.org/eapro/MDG_Profile_Singapore_2013.pdf.